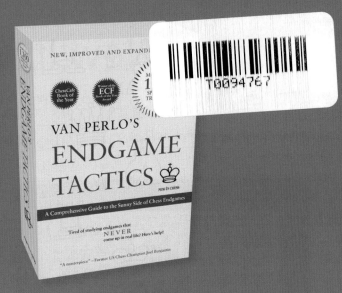

Download the New In Chess app:

- get early access to every issue
- follow every move on the built-in board

Read New In Chess on your tablet, smartphone or Windows PC, two weeks before the printed edition is available, and replay all the moves in the interactive chess viewer

You can now download the digital edition of New In Chess on your tablet, phone or PC/notebook and read all the stories immediately after publication. By simply tapping on the games you can replay the moves on the interactive chessviewer. So from now on you don't need a board and set to fully enjoy what top grandmasters have to say about their games! The New In Chess app installs in seconds, has all the right features and is easy to operate. We have made an entire issue available as a FREE DOWNLOAD.

The chess magazine that moves
Now available for iOS, Android and Windows

NEW FRITZ-TRAINER DVDs

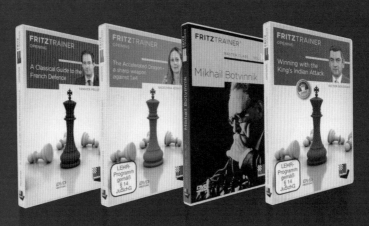

YANNICK PELLETIER:
A CLASSICAL GUIDE TO THE FRENCH DEFENCE

GM Yannick Pelletier is a specialist of the French Defence, and believes that the most efficient way to understand its ideas, plans, and typical structures is to study classical lines. He offers you a repertoire that is based on well-established lines that have been tried and tested for decades and that have proven their validity. He illustrates these lines with thematic games. This DVD is an interactive video training course. At key moments, the five times Suisse champion pauses and asks you to find and play the best move. He then gives feedback to the moves that you entered on the board. The database with illustrative games will also help you to understand and play the French better and better. The author has selected all games in the database carefully and annotated most of them. Video running time: 7 hours 27 minutes (English and French).

29,90 €

NADEZHDA KOSINTSEVA:
THE ACCELERATED DRAGON -
A SHARP WEAPON AGAINST 1.e4

Nadezhda Kosintseva has won Olympic gold no less than six times - twice with the Russian team and four times as the best player on her board. Her first Fritztrainer DVD is dedicated to her favorite opening: the Accelerated Dragon (1.e4 c5 2.Nf3 Nc6 3.d4 cxd4 4.Nxd4 g6). From the fifth move, White is faced with the choice of playing either the popular Maroczy bind structure with 5.c4 or the "Open System" with 5.Nc3. Kosintseva has more than one attractive answer for Black on her DVD for both playing styles! The focus is clearly on a comprehensive and in-depth presentation of both main variations and the remaining sidelines, but the DVD also covers typical strategic ideas like the breakthroughs d7-d5 and b7-b5 and the classic Sicilian exchange sacrifice ...Rxc3 followed by ...Nxe4. Let the former top player inspire you and bring some momentum to your opening repertoire - with this complete repertoire against 1.e4!

29,90 €

MASTER CLASS 10:
MIKHAIL BOTVINNIK

Mikhail Botvinnik became World Champion in 1948 and remained at the top until 1963. His influence on the development of top-level chess was enormous, for it was only with Botvinnik that systematic and rather scientific work on chess began. He studied openings and looked at the middlegame structures which typically arose from them and developed successful strategies to deal with the positions. His strategic approach is apparent throughout Botvinnik's work. Many of his games were part of the basic training of young chess players in strategy and endgame management at the time of the "Soviet Chess School" and are still of inestimable value today as a yardstick for successful play. Let our team of experts show you how to successfully play certain openings as well as patterns that exist in certain structures, how to find tactical solutions and how to win endgames according to established rules. Video running time: 7 hours (English). Includes all of Botvinnik's games, tournament tables, a short biography and much more. Watch demo video!

29,90 €

VIKTOR BOLOGAN:
WINNING WITH THE KING'S INDIAN ATTACK

The King Indian Attack was a favourite of chess legend Bobby Fischer, who was known for his aggressive play and for his desire to win every game! He scored 8.5/9 with it, leaving a series of illustrative games in his wake. The "KIA" is mainly reached against the French Defence (1.e4 e6 2.d3) and the Sicilian when Black plays 2... e6, but it can also arise from the Réti opening when Black plays ...e6 and ....d5. 30 years ago, the King's Indian Attack was still considered an original means of avoiding theoretical battles. Today, however, the "KIA" gets the standard opening treatment, with the fight for the center now postponed to the middlegame and some lines very well-trodden. The opening is full of positional and tactical ideas and often holds unpleasant surprises for your opponent!

29,90 €

ChessBase GmbH · News: en.chessbase.com · CB Shop: shop.chessbase.com
CHESSBASE DEALER: NEW IN CHESS · P.O. Box 1093 · NL-1810 KB Alkmaar
phone (+31)72 5127137 · fax (+31)72 5158234 · WWW.NEWINCHESS.COM

'There is something about nearly every opening one can think of.'
– British Chess Magazine

128

NEW IN CHESS
Yearbook
A QUARTERLY PUBLICATION

McShane paints the Ruy Lopez in KID colours

★ The full story behind Magnus' new anti-Sicilian weapon

★ Shakh Mamedyarov defies Kramnik in the Catalan

★ Anish Giri wins from 0.00 in the Caro-Kann

★ Alexandr Predke on confusing Black in the Classical QI

★ And dozens of other ideas to refresh your repertoire

CHESS OPENING NEWS

paperback | 256 pages | € 29.95

With answers to urgent questions such as:

- What does Ponomariov recommend against the Najdorf with 6.♗g5?
- How can the quietest lines in the Moscow Sicilian result in very sharp battles?
- Why is 7.♕f3 in the Taimanov Sicilian easier for White?
- Is the Fegatello still alive?
- Has the QI with 4...♗a6 and 5...c5 been refuted?
- Has Magnus Carlsen found a hole in the Berlin Wall?
- How is Black doing in the Four Knights Sicilian?
- What is the idea behind 6.g4 in the Taimanov Sicilian?
- What is the story behind Magnus Carlsen's sensational new Closed Sicilian line?
- Which new dangerous set-up makes Black's life difficult in the French Steinitz?
- How does Adhiban turn 3...c5 against the Advance Caro-Kann into a winning weapon?
- What are the dangers for Black in the Laznicka Variation of the Scandinavian?
- What is the latest news in the Nimzowitsch Petroff?
- What is the status of the Anti-Berlin with 8.♗xc6?
- Can Black hold in the Poisoned Pawn Steinitz?
- What is Luke McShane's key to success in the Neo-Steinitz Variation with black?
- How good is Shakhriyar Mamedyarov's 7...♕d6 in the Catalan with 6...dxc4 ?
- With which sharp system in the Classical Nimzo-Indian can Black set fire on board?
- How serious is the quiet 10.h3 as an attempt to get an advantage in the Fianchetto Grünfeld?
- What is Ding Liren's improvement in the Steinitz' C-K?
- How do specialists like Levon Aronian and Ding Liren treat the Flohr/Mikenas?
- What is currently the most dynamic line in the London?
- What is the latest gambit idea in the Symmetrical English for White?

Now available in a digital interactive edition
Please have a look at the free apps

'I view chess as an incredible world of opportunity.'

8 Only a pawn in their game
A Rapid & Blitz tournament in Abidjan may have been the preamble to an African leg of the Grand Chess Tour in 2019.

10 NIC's Café
Finally Lennox Lewis and Vitaly Klitschko will step into the ring for a revenge fight… on the chess board.

12 Your Move
Why did Reuben Fine lose an easily won game against Samuel Reshevsky in Pasadena 86 years ago?

14 Mamedyarov in top form
A graphic about the recent rise of Azerbaijan's number one.

15 Fair & Square
Don Henley reveals that not everyone was thrilled when The Eagles recorded their hit 'Desperado'.

16 The benefits of wisdom
Magnus Carlsen was the undeniable headliner in Biel, but the indisputable star was 'Shakh' Mamedyarov, who finished one and a half points ahead of the World Champion. Nico Georgiadis reports from an unusual perspective.

23 Celeb64: Dizzy Gillespie

38 The Ticket
Genna Sosonko wrote a fine addendum to his latest book, *Evil-Doer, Half a Century with Viktor Kortchnoi*.

45 Maximize Your Tactics
Find the right moves.

46 Short Stories
When one of his opponents in the FIDE presidential elections posted a combination that he was proud of, Nigel Short decided it was time to fulfil an old promise to our readers.

52 Secrets of Opening Surprises
Shirov's shocker in the French Rubinstein.

56 Nepo dominates Dortmund
In a seven-round sprint, Ian Nepomniachtchi finished a full point ahead of his closest pursuers. Vladimir 'Mr Dortmund' Kramnik fought like a lion, but took too many risks.

76 Chess Pattern Recognition
Capa's bishop sac against Bogoljubow in Moscow 1925 is a classic that remains relevant today.

78 The Blitz Whisperer
Maxim Dlugy examines Anatoly Karpov's inimitable style… in blitz!

86 Sadler on Books
Matthew Sadler reviews a rich and varied bouquet of new books.

92 Judit Polgar
Studies are aesthetically pleasing and intellectually challenging, but they also help you become a better player, as Judit Polgar shows.

96 Going digital
Hans Ree muses about his initiation, years ago, into the digital age.

98 Hammer blows in Helsingor
Jan Timman was impressed by the games that Jon-Ludvig Hammer played to win the Xtracon Open, including one 'that his friend Magnus Carlsen would have been proud of'.

106 Just Checking
Which three people would Cristian Chirila like to invite for dinner?

CONTRIBUTORS TO THIS ISSUE
Erwin l'Ami, Jeroen Bosch, Cristian Chirila, Maxim Dlugy, Nico Georgiadis, Anish Giri, John Henderson, Dylan McClain, Ian Nepomniachtchi, Maxim Notkin, Arthur van de Oudeweetering, Judit Polgar, Hans Ree, Matthew Sadler, Nigel Short, Genna Sosonko, Jan Timman

ALINA L'AMI

Only a Pawn in Their Game

More than any other piece, the pawn in chess is used widely as a metaphor in the media, in politics, and even the title of a 1963 tribute song by Bob Dylan, Only a Pawn in their Game, after the assassination of civil rights leader Medgar Evers. The image above, captured by globetrotting chess photographer Alina l'Ami, features the hands of IMs Oladapho Adu (Nigeria) and Andrew Kayonde (Zambia), with the focus being on a pawn in their game from the recent Côte d'Ivoire Rapid & Blitz Invitational at the luxurious 5-star Tiama Hotel in Abidjan, one of the strongest and richest tournaments of its kind ever to be held on the African continent, that was won by Egyptian GM Bassem Amin. Inspired by the Grand Chess

Tour, the Fédération Ivoirienne des Echecs teamed up with the Kasparov Chess Foundation to showcase the very best of African chess. And thanks to sponsorship from Vivendi SA – the French mass media backers of the Paris Grand Chess Tour event – there was a $15,000 prize pool that was distributed based on the combined standings of both the rapid and blitz events, with formats played in line with the GCT time controls and standards. Thousands of spectators worldwide tuned in to the live stream and GM commentary of the event that was provided by the producers from St. Louis in the USA – and it all proved to be such a success, there's now talk of the tournament being 'upgraded' to becoming part of the full GCT circuit. ∎

NIC's Café

We'll meet again

Back in 2003, it was billed as 'Battle of the Titans', as Lennox Lewis and Vitali Klitschko prepared to go toe to toe in one of the biggest professional boxing matches of the era, with all four main heavyweight titles on the line.

But in the run-up to the epic bout at the Staples Center in Los Angeles, the media was bemused by the pre-fight preparations from the two pugilists. In the absence of the usual trash talk – and with defending champion Lewis revealing he was playing chess as part

Vitali Klitschko-Lennox Lewis: this time it will be different.

of his training to help stay mentally sharp for his Ukrainian challenger – when the media went to Klitschko's camp for his response, he did so, with: 'First I beat Lewis on the chess board, and then we meet in the ring.'

There was no chess, but Lewis won the controversial fight after being behind on points when doctors ordered the referee to call a halt at the end of the sixth round as blood poured from cuts around Klitschko's eyes. Sadly, there never was a rematch.

Both heavyweight legends have now long retired, but earlier this year, media rumours started swirling that Lewis and Klitschko would be returning to the ring after 15 years, to finally have that rematch. Now the date has been set: the two will climb through the ropes in Kiev in the first week in October. Only this time, it will be a battle of brains, not brawn.

Klitschko, now the mayor of the Ukrainian capital, which will be hosting the annual WBC convention at the time, has finally persuaded his

rival to give him a second shot. As Lewis clarified: 'We are going to play a chess match inside a boxing ring. We are too old now to be pulling on the gloves again.'

The first world title match ...

Rex Sinquefield is always on a mission. The latest from the St. Louis chess patron was to commemorate one of the venues in his hometown where the first official World Championship Match between Wilhelm Steinitz and Johannes Zukertort took place. The three-leg US match began on January 11, 1886, with five games played in New York City, then the next four in St. Louis, with the final eleven games being held in New Orleans.

But the exact location for one of the two St. Louis venues is still clouded in some mystery. The games were played during the day at the Harmonie Hall and at night in the Chess, Checkers and Whist Club, but no one has discovered the exact address for the latter. In 1906, the Harmonie Hall was repurposed as a warehouse and rebranded as the Butler Brothers Building, with the impressive, locally quarried red-brick property on the western edge of downtown on 18th Street now listed in the National Register of Historic Places.

In early August, the building received another accolade, as Rex Sinquefield, surrounded by participants of the Grand Chess Tour, unveiled a massive new banner to

The old Harmonie Hall building today with an outsized post-it note that reminds us of the historic match.

commemorate that first 1886 World Chess Championship that had a brief stop in St. Louis.

... and the latest

From the first location for a World Championship match, we nicely segue to the latest, as also in early August, Agon/World Chess finally announced the London location for the upcoming match between defending champion Magnus Carlsen and his US challenger, Fabiano Caruana. Live streaming from the World Chess Club bar in Moscow, World Chess CEO Ilya Merenzon

No doubt The College will look slightly different in November.

revealed that an equally imposing and historic building, The College, 12-42 Southampton Row in Holborn, London, is set to stage the match.

Formerly the home of the internationally renowned Central Saint Martins College of Art and Design, The College is a large site with period Victorian halls and interconnecting rooms that is now being utilized as a space to hire for major international events. The match will run 9-28 November and, if you want to be a part of chess history, tickets have gone on sale at Ticketmaster.

A game for the ages

This summer cinephiles celebrated the centennial of Ingmar Bergman's (1918-2007) birth with retrospectives of the legendary Swedish film-maker's masterworks shown in arthouses across the world.

The key scene from *The Seventh Seal*: a game of chess with Death.

Bergman's films are as full of joy and lust for life as they are with probing psychological fragility and agonizing over the meaning of existence in a universe abandoned by an indifferent creator – and none more so than the movie the director admitted was the closest of all to his heart, the existential classic *The Seventh Seal* (1957).

It depicts the disillusioned and exhausted Antonius Block (Max von Sydow) returning from his Crusades campaign, only to encounter the Grim Reaper (Bengt Ekerot) on a dank and desolate Nordic pebble beach. To forestall his impending fate, the lengthy key scene involves the medieval knight challenging Death to a game of chess for his very soul – and those visually stunning chess scenes are hailed by cinematic academics and enthusiasts alike to be some of the most famous images shot in film history.

The Conversation

O ften referred to as 'a sanity life-saver' for those travelling or perhaps living overseas, the BBC World Service (BBCWS) provides impartial news reports and analysis in English.

They also broadcast some very interesting discussion shows. 'The Conversation', hosted by Kim Chakanesta, presents a conversation over the airwaves between two women from different cultures about their paths to success. A recent episode featured two leading women who have broken records and barriers

playing chess: Judit Polgar and Hou Yifan.

The near half-hour episode 'Chess Grandmasters' heard the two highest-ranked women players of all-time discuss with the host the many pitfalls they faced while trying to make it in the ruthlessly competitive, male-dominated world of chess. Among the issues that came to the fore during the lively to and fro were Polgar's problematic early attempt to play for Hungary in the 1992 Olympiad, and Hou's pairings protest in Gibraltar 2017 that led to her deliberately throwing her final round game.

Hou Yifan and Judit Polgar on the ruthlessly competitive, male-dominated world of chess.

Anyone anywhere can access the full interview on the iPlayer (www.bbc.co.uk/programmes/p0290t8h) for up to a year, and it is also available for download as a podcast.

'Go Home' Office

I mmigration-wise, Britain is in a bit of a mess. First it was an ill-fated government billboard campaign, telling illegal immigrants to 'Go home or face arrest', followed by Brexit, and then the Windrush scandal with many long-standing British subjects from the Caribbean being wrongly detained, and even wrongly deported by the Home Office.

And now the latest embarrassment to be exposed by the UK media involved a young chess prodigy, 9-year-old Shreyas Royal, hailed as being Britain's 'greatest chess

prospect in a generation', who was told by the Home Office that he had to pack up his bags and return to India in September with his family.

Born in India, Shreyas grew up in south London and is among the top players in the world in his age group, with his case turning on Britain's strict enforcement of new immigration laws, the renewal of his father's work visa (but only if he could earn more than £120,000 a year), and even on one government junior minister questioning whether chess is a sport or not (it isn't, apparently).

'It is just bureaucracy gone mad,' proclaimed Dominic Lawson, the president of the English Chess Federation. The chess community swiftly moved into action, with wordsmith Lawson penning a letter that implored home secretary Sajid Javid to step in. Even former Monty Python star John Cleese chimed in, expressing his indignation.

Thankfully, common sense – not to mention a viral media campaign – prevailed, with the Home Office in mid-August finally bowing to the inevitable eleventh hour change of mind in an email to his father, Jitendra Singh.

Shreyas Royal helped Magnus Carlsen with his first move during last year's London Classic and may well do so again in the coming world title match in the British capital.

'We are very happy and Shreyas is very happy,' said Singh. 'He jumped up on the sofa when he heard the news.' ■

Playing bridge with Alekhine

In regard to the missing game score for Fine vs. Reshevsky, Pasadena 1932, and Aidan Woodger's remark in New In Chess 2018/5, p. 12 ('In the absence of the game score, a contemporary account of the circumstances would be invaluable'), a short article in the August 1949 *California Chess News*, by Harry Borochow, one of the participants in that tournament, adds a bit of information about the game. Borochow writes: 'Fine lost two very valuable points, which he need not have done in the tournament. He had a very easily won game with Samuel Reshevsky, and failed to show up at the adjourned time. He had been playing bridge with Alekhine and others until about three o'clock in the morning and no one woke him up to appear for the appointment with Reshevsky, whereupon the clock ticked the valuable moments away until Reshevsky won by default.'

Ed Tassinari
Scarsdale, New York, USA

Endgame theory in action

At the beginning of August 2018, Anish Giri came to Hamburg to train endgames with me. We mostly concentrated on rook endings and he found one major mistake, which throws new light onto the defence of a typical setup:

This position (after 47.♔h3) is from the game Heinemann-Zelbel, Germany Bundesliga 2014. Such endings with a pawn on g5 are not so well dealt with in the literature. Play now continued:

47...♖a4? A typical mistake. The rook moves behind the passed pawn, when in fact it should stay flexible. I had published extensive analysis by Spanish IM Arizmendi in my *Endgame Corner* at ChessCafe.com in 2004 and on the schachbundesliga.de website in 2014. I believed that Black draws this way as well.

In fact the rook should stay flexible with 47...♖c4! (or ♖d4/♖b4) 48.a6 (48.♖b7 ♖a4 49.♖b5 – the rook on the side is less effective as Black can choose whether to activate the king via f8 and e7 or go for counterplay with ...f6) 48...♖c6 49.♔g3 ♔g7 50.♔f4 ♖e6

This cut-off is a suggestion of Anish Giri to defend based on Onischuk's draw against Urkedal in Khanty-Mansiysk 2017, e.g. 51.♖a8 ♔h7 52.f3 ♔g7 53.a7 ♖a6=.

48.a6 ♔g7 49.f4 ♖a3+

49...♖xf4?! is met by 50.♖c7 ♖a4 51.a7 followed by White's king invading on the queenside.

50.♔g2

In 2014 I had written: 'Now only a miracle can save Black'. During our session Anish proved that there will

be no miracle contrary to what I had believed for almost four years.

50...♖a2+?!

After 50...♖a4!? 51.♔f3 ♔f8

there is no reciprocal zugzwang as White can triangulate, which I had missed: 52.♔e2! (after the direct 52.♖a8+?! ♔g7 53.♔e3 ♔h7 54.♔d3? ♖xf4 55.♖f8 ♔g7 56.a7 ♔xf8 57.a8♕+ ♔g7 58.♕a1+ ♔g8 59.♕e1 ♖g4= Black's fortress cannot be broken. 52.♔e3 ♔g7 – now with White to move he will have to start the triangulation all over again, because after 53.♔d3? ♖xf4 54.♔c3 ♖xh4 he is one crucial tempo short compared to the game) 52...♔g7 53.♔e3!. This was Anish's move. Now White wins as we reach the same zugzwang position as in the game after 52.♔e3.

51.♔f3 ♖a4 52.♔e3

Black is in a deadly zugzwang.

52...♔g8 53.♔d3 ♔g7

After 53...♖xf4 54.♖b7 ♖a4 55.a7 White will eventually bring the king to a8, as Black is paralysed and has no counterplay whatsoever.

54.♔c3 ♖xf4 55.♖b7 ♖xh4 56.♖b4 ♖h3+ 57.♔b2 ♖h2+ 58.♔b3

58.♔a3 immediately is the way, and Heinemann played it after repeating once.

58...♖h1 59.♔a2 ♖h2+ 60.♔a3! ♖h1 61.♖a4! ♖a1+ 62.♔b4 ♖b1+

Now the king has to move into the shadow with **63.♔a5!**

63.♔c5? was played in the game, which was drawn later. The winning method is as follows:

63...♖b8 64.♖c4 Now 64...f6 or ...f5 lose due to 65.♖c7+, but Black has one final defensive attempt:

64...♖h8!?

64...h4 65.♖xh4 f6 66.♖b4!+–, a crucial tempo-move, not giving Black time to create a passed g-pawn. Here it matters that the king is on a5 and not on c5, as Black doesn't have a check on c8.

65.a7 h4 66.♖xh4!

66.♖b4? allows Black a miraculous escape: 66...♖a8 67.♔a6 h3 68.♖b2 ♖c8 69.♖b8 h2 70.♖xc8 h1♕ 71.a8♕ ♕a1+, when despite being a rook up White cannot stop the perpetual, as his major pieces are too deep in the opponent's territory.

66...♖xh4 67.a8♕

Arizmendi had left the question open if this is a fortress or not. In 2004 I had claimed it to be a draw, but in 2014 I understood it was winning, which was later confirmed by the 7-men tablebase: White mates in 52 moves.

67...♖c4 An attempt to build a floating barrier along the c-file, but with the help of good king-queen teamwork White is able to break it.

68.♔b5 ♖c1 69.♔b4 ♖c2 70.♔b3

Write to us
New In Chess, P.O. Box 1093
1810 KB Alkmaar, The Netherlands
or e-mail: editors@newinchess.com
Letters may be edited or abridged

♖c1 71.♔b2 ♖c5 72.♕d8 ♖c6 73.♕d7 ♖c4 74.♕b5 ♖c8 75.♕a6! Taking away all the light squares from the rook and after...

75...♖c5 76.♕f6+ ♔g8 77.♕d8+! ♔h7 77...♔g7 78.♕d4+!. **78.♕e7**

... Black is forced to allow the white king to cross the c-file and eventually cross other files and ranks until reaching f8.

And so Anish refuted my defence by triangulation, but fortunately for the defender he found another solid setup, with Black's rook on e6 instead of on the a-file, which is well worth knowing.

Karsten Müller
Hamburg, Germany

Arch hypermodernist

In New In Chess 2018/5 (page 15) you quote Ernst Grünfeld and write 'The German arch hypermodernist ...'.

Most people believe he was a chess-player from Austria. He was born in Vienna (his father coming to Vienna from Silesia, his mother coming from Bohemia) and lived in Vienna up to his death. A detailed account of his life is published in the book *Geniales Schach im Wiener Kaffeehaus 1750 – 1918* (Edition Steinbauer, Vienna 2017), written by Michael Ehn.

Werner Reif
Klosterneuburg, Austria

Onlooker

In New In Chess 2050/3, I fully expect to be an onlooker in a photo and not identified.

But on page 60 of New In Chess 2018/4, you fail to point out in the 1944 photo the illustrious Edward Lasker (far left), Al Horowitz (right of Steiner) and the great Frank Marshall himself, who has posthumously ended the Spanish Opening as we knew it (stooping on right), just months from his death.

IM Anthony Saidy
Los Angeles, CA, USA

COLOPHON

PUBLISHER: Allard Hoogland
EDITOR-IN-CHIEF:
Dirk Jan ten Geuzendam
HONORARY EDITOR: Jan Timman
CONTRIBUTING EDITOR: Anish Giri
EDITORS: Peter Boel, René Olthof
PRODUCTION: Joop de Groot
TRANSLATORS: Sarah Hurst, Ken Neat, Piet Verhagen
SALES AND ADVERTISING: Remmelt Otten

PHOTOS AND ILLUSTRATIONS IN THIS ISSUE:
Alina I'Ami, Simon Bohnenblust, Fred Lucas,
Hartmut Metz, Lennart Ootes, Georgios Souleidis

COVER PHOTO: Shakhriyar
Mamedyarov: Lennart Ootes

© No part of this magazine may be reproduced, stored in a retrieval system or transmitted in any form or by any means, recording or otherwise, without the prior permission of the publisher.

NEW IN CHESS
P.O. BOX 1093
1810 KB ALKMAAR
THE NETHERLANDS

PHONE: 00-31-(0)72-51 27 137
SUBSCRIPTIONS: nic@newinchess.com
EDITORS: editors@newinchess.com
ADVERTISING: otten@newinchess.com

WWW.NEWINCHESS.COM

Mamedyarov in Top Form

Shakhriyar Mamedyarov of Azerbaijan has always showed great promise, and sometimes his results have lived up to expectations. But he has also been plagued with inconsistency.

Though he has been among the world's best players for more than a decade, his ranking has bounced around and there have been times when he was not even the first or second best player in his country.

In the last 18 months, however, Mamedyarov has found his form and his ranking has risen to a career best, even touching No. 2 for several months. At the Biel tournament in late July and early August, he demonstrated just how formidable he has become with a bravura performance – winning by 1½ points ahead of a field that included Magnus Carlsen, the World Champion.   *DYLAN LOEB McCLAIN*

World rankings of top players from Azerbaijan

Shakhriyar Mamedyarov   Teimour Radjabov   Vugar Gashimov*

*Gashimov died at age 27 on Jan. 11, 2014, while receiving treatment for a brain tumor.

Quality of play: Mamedyarov vs. Carlsen

Percentage of each player's moves that matched the first preference of Stockfish (versions 6 through 9) during each tournament.

The data is based on research by Ken Regan, an associate professor of computer science at the University of Buffalo, who is also an international master. (Dr. Regan's research is used by the World Chess Federation to try to identify possible cheaters.) The data does not 'normalize' for the difficulty of positions and includes only tournaments played at standard, or slow, time controls since 2015.

Mamedyarov
Carlsen

Rank (out of 125,000 player performances in FIDE-rated tournaments evaluated since 2015)

Tournament	Score	Rank
Moscow Grand Prix, 2017	72.2	23
Sinquefield Cup, 2017	68.0	169
Tata Steel, 2018	67.9	177
3rd Gashimov Memorial, 2016	67.5	215
Biel Chess Festival, 2018	67.0	270
5th Gashimov Memorial, 2018	66.8	291
Reykjavik Open, 2015	66.3	370
European Club Cup, 2016	66.0	440
Grenke Chess Classic, 2017	65.7	501
Biel Chess Festival, 2018	64.9	763
Tata Steel, 2016	64.9	783
Isle of Man Masters, 2017	64.6	878

Mamedyarov's most important tournament victories

2003 and 2005
World Junior Championship (Mamedyarov is the only player to win the title twice)

2006
Aeroflot Open (tied for first with Viktor Bologan, Krishnan Sasikiran and Baadur Jobava)

Hoogeveen Essent (tied for first with Judit Polgar)

2009
Mainz Ordix Rapid Open

2010
President's Cup Baku (tied for first with Vladimir Kramnik and Gata Kamsky)

Tal Memorial Moscow (tied for first with Levon Aronian and Sergey Karjakin)

2013
World Rapid Championship

FIDE Grand Prix tournament, Beijing

2014
Tal Memorial Moscow

2016
Gashimov Memorial Shamkir

2017
Gashimov Memorial Shamkir

FIDE Grand Prix (first after four tournaments)

2018
Biel Chess Festival

Roger Lowenstein: 'Being right on a stock had something of the purity of a perfect move in chess; it had an intellectual resonance.' *(The American writer in his authorized biography of billionaire stockmarket guru Warren Buffett, 'Buffett: The Making of an American Capitalist')*

Richard Branson: 'There is a big difference between a calculated risk and a foolish gamble. Business is like a giant game of chess: you have to make strategic moves, and learn quickly from your mistakes.' *(The entrepreneur, writing recently on his website, on how his Virgin business empire only grew because of bold risks he made in the markets)*

Rustam Kasimdzhanov: 'A good second is everything from a psychological consultant to an expert on nutrition.' *(World Chess Championship Challenger Fabiano Caruana's second, interviewed on Chesspro.ru)*

Jorge Luis Borges: 'Chess is one of the means we have to save culture, such as Latin, the study of the humanities, the reading of classics, the laws of versification, ethics. Chess is now replaced by football, boxing or tennis, which are games of fools, not of intellectuals.' *(The chess-playing Argentine short-story writer, essayist and poet, during a 1981 interview)*

Michael Klonovsky: 'Chess, considered as a test for the intellect, must be unimportant; or else surely there would have been more female grand-masters.' *(The German political journalist and commentator)*

Don Henley: 'They had brought chess boards with them. Each pair of players would set up a chessboard between them, and when we weren't doing any takes, they would play. Once in a while I would hear a remark from the back: "You know, I don't feel like a desperado."' *(The Eagles drummer and vocalist during a 2015 interview with his friend Billy Joel, at New York's 92nd Street Y, on the stressful time recording the supergroup's hit 'Desperado' in London with bored members of the London Symphony Orchestra)*

Ljubomir Ljubojevic: 'I have won many games that have not made me happy and when I lose, I am also not happy. My friends ask "so when are you happy?" That's the way chess is; you are happy only rarely; the rest is grief.'

Leon Wildes: 'It's a game of chess... and there are a number of moves we'd have to make.' *(The noted New York immigration attorney, in his 2016 best-selling book 'John Lennon vs. The U.S.A.', recalling his first conversation in 1972 with the Beatles legend and his wife, Yoko Ono, and having to explain the legal technicalities behind what turned out to be the most bitterly contested deportation case in US history)*

Hannu Rajaniemi: 'I'm not much of a chess player, but there is an aspect of the game that I find fascinating. After a while, you can almost see lines of force between the pieces. Areas of danger where it is physically impossible to move pieces into. Clouds of possibility, forbidden zones.' *(The Finnish science fiction author, in his second sci-fi novel, 'The Fractal Prince')*

Daniel Negreanu: 'New fun goal for me is to get my chess.com rating from 946 to 1200 in a year. Not sure if that's hard or not?' *(Tweeted recently by the poker superstar, as he charts his continued progress after catching the chess bug)*

David Bronstein: 'If you have made a mistake or committed an inaccuracy there is no need to become annoyed and to think that everything is lost. You have to reorientate yourself quickly and find a new plan in the new situation.'

David Mitchell: 'We nerdy kids used to hide away at school and made a secret society with the chess club.' *(The British comedian/writer/author in his award-winning sitcom, Peep Show, written in conjunction with his co-star, Robert Webb)*

Shakh Mamedyarov and the benefits of wisdom

Masterful victory in Biel ahead of Magnus Carlsen

Magnus Carlsen was the undeniable headliner of the 51st Biel Chess Festival, but the indisputable star was Shakhriyar Mamedyarov. Consistent, controlled and striking at the right moments, the Azeri put in a jaw-dropping 2921 performance to finish one and a half points ahead of the World Champion. Our man on the spot was **NICO GEORGIADIS**. The Swiss GM finished clear last, and from this unusual perspective the local hero provides a fascinating and insightful account. Be ready for drama, or what he calls a 'once-in-a-lifetime experience'.

LENNART OOTES

Shakhriyar Mamedyarov won five games and drew the other five.
'I used to play more aggressively, while now you might say I play more wisely.'

When Biel tournament director Yannick Pelletier contacted me at the beginning of this year to lay out his plans to make the 2018 edition of the Grandmaster tournament a world-class event and tell me that they wanted me to participate as a representative of the host country, I accepted the invitation without thinking twice. But one month later, when Yannick told me in another email that the first top players who had confirmed their participation were Magnus Carlsen and Maxime Vachier-Lagrave, I started to grasp the magnitude of the challenge ahead. Once the complete field was known, I understood that I should probably start working on chess again in order to avoid 10 consecutive losses!

Because I had been focusing on my studies, I hadn't been working on chess, and to be honest, I didn't feel very motivated to do so. Obviously, this invitation brought about a mental turnaround. I suddenly had an abundance of motivation!

Even though I still had to complete some major assignments for my Bachelor degree this summer, I tried to prepare as well as possible and worked not only on openings, but also studied my opponents' games, especially those of the World Champion. I also tried to get into gear by solving at least one study per day and playing regular training games against my friend and coach GM Mihajlo Stojanovic and other friends.

The Swiss Championship had been scheduled just before Biel. On the

one hand this was a bit unfortunate, since it would be quite tiring to play 19 games in just 21 days. On the other hand, it was a good chance for me to get some practice, since my last tournament had been the European Team Championship in Crete, in November 2017. Regrettably, I came down with a bad cold at the end of the Swiss championship, which resulted in a disastrous last-round loss against GM Joe Gallagher with the white pieces.

Luckily, during the one night that I spent at home, I was nursed by my loving family and as result arrived in Biel in quite decent physical shape, considering that the previous day I had barely been able to breathe. I managed to sleep well and felt ready for the first game, as Black, against Shakhriyar Mamedyarov. However,

'Once the complete field was known, I understood that I should probably start working on chess again in order to avoid 10 consecutive losses!'

health was not a decisive factor in that game at all. My opponent surprised me early in the opening with an interesting new idea to which I didn't react accurately, and after some accurate moves by Shakh, I soon ended up in a bad position and lost.

Since I didn't have any great expectations regarding points, this loss didn't affect me much. I knew in advance that such games would happen and that I would have to look at every game as a new opportunity to play a world-class player. Every time I should just give my best and try to fight back as much as possible. For the same reason, it didn't bother me that I started with two Blacks, the second one against Peter Svidler. This time I guessed the opening correctly and had quite a pleasant position out of the opening. As the game continued,

I started spending too much time on quite easy moves, a bad habit of mine, which troubled me in almost every game. I've been trying to get rid of this time-trouble 'illness' for a long time, but unfortunately, my recent lack of practice made it even worse. Suffice it to say that it's my main problem and that I'll have to keep working on it. If one has such an apparent weakness, opponents at this level will always try to exploit this weakness. I will get back to this point later.

Going back to the game, with little time on the clock I erred and after the time trouble found myself in an almost lost position. However, I managed to find some good defensive moves, including a piece sacrifice, but two moves later I unfortunately missed something that was not too difficult to spot.

Peter Svidler
Nico Georgiadis
Biel 2018 (2)

position after 42.♔h1

42...♗xf3! The only chance.
I had calculated 42...♕d2 43.♖e5! ♕c1+ 44.♔h2 ♕f4+ 45.♔g1 ♕c1+ 46.♔f2 ♕d2+ 47.♔g3 ♕f4+ 48.♔h4, and White wins, because Black is running out of checks.
And after 42...♗d5 43.♖e5! Black lacks counterplay.
43.gxf3 ♖xf3 43...♕d5 won't work because of 44.♘e5 ♖xf3 (after 44...♖f6 45.♕c7! ♖xf3 46.♘xf3 ♕xf3+ 47.♔g1 there is no perpetual check either) 45.♕g6+!.
44.♕e6

44...♕d3? Just overlooking White's next move. If I had seen it, I would have gone for 44...♖xh3+ 45.♔g2 ♖h5 (after 45...♕d3?, 46.♘f6+ is a killer), when 46.b3! is probably the best move, since all other moves give Black decent drawing chances. The endgame after 46...♕d5+ 47.♔g3!? ♕xe6 48.♖xe6 ♖h1 49.♔f4 ♖b1 50.♖xa6 ♖xb3 51.a5 is probably winning for White.
44...♕f4 is another move, but again

Nico Georgiadis: 'I knew in advance that such games would happen and that I would have to look at every game as a new opportunity to play a world-class player.'

White has a strong reply: 45.♖e3!, and there is no move after 45...♖f1+ 46.♔g2.

Finally, 44...♕xa4 45.♘e5 ♖f6 46.♕d5 ♕h4 47.♕d3+ ♔g8 48.♖e3 also looks very promising for White.

45.♘e3!

Now, White has it all under control.

45...bxa4 46.♔g2 ♖f6 47.♕d5 ♕g6+ 48.♔h1 ♖f2 49.♖g1 ♕h6 50.♖g3

50...♕f6 50...♖xb2 doesn't work in view of 51.♕e4+ g6 52.♘f5!, and wins. The best try was 50...♕f4, even though the position looks lost after 51.♕h5+ ♔g8 52.♕e8+ ♕f8 53.♕xf8+ ♔xf8 54.♘c4 ♖c2 55.♖g4.

51.♕d3+ ♔h8 52.♘g4! ♕c6+ 53.♔g1 ♖xb2 54.♕d8+ ♔h7 55.♕h4+ ♔g8 56.♘h6+

Black resigned.

I was obviously disappointed with this result, but at least I had managed to resist for quite a long time, which gave me some hope for the next game with the white pieces against David Navara. Once again, the opening was a disappointment, because I couldn't remember anything and played a

natural-looking move after which White was already somewhat worse. Later, I decided to give the queen for a rook and a minor piece with David's first-round game in mind, when he couldn't handle this type of material distribution against the World Champion. Even though I was sure that the queen sacrifice was not entirely correct, I preferred this type of position against precisely this opponent to one in which he could press me in the long run. Indeed, it turned out to be a good idea, since David soon started to lose control of the position. Unfortunately, when he did so, I was already down to two minutes on the clock... I missed quite a good chance to even play for a win, and in the wild complications David outplayed me without problems in my time-trouble. Yet another loss was booked!

However, the highlight of the third round was a very convincing victory by the later tournament winner.

NOTES BY
Nico Georgiadis

Shakhriyar Mamedyarov
Maxime Vachier-Lagrave
Biel 2018 (3)
English Opening, Symmetrical Variation

1.♘f3

Usually, Mamedyarov's main weapon is 1.d4, but in his first two white games, he surprised me and Vachier-Lagrave with 1.c4 and 1.♘f3, before switching back to 1.d4.

1...c5 2.c4 ♘c6 3.♘c3 e5 4.e3 ♘f6 5.d4 e4 6.♘e5 g6

7.g4!? Shakh was ready for this line and uncorked this strong idea, which has been played before (the first time in a blitz game between Movsesian and Ponomariov), but which Maxime hadn't looked at before the game.
7.♗e2 and 7.♖b1 are the alternatives.

7...h6 White is a bit better after 7...♗g7 8.g5 ♘h5 9.♘xe4 0-0 10.♗g2 cxd4 11.exd4 ♘xe5 12.dxe5 ♗xe5 13.0-0 due to Black's weak d-pawn.

8.♗g2 ♗g7 9.h3!?

This is the novelty Shakh had prepared.

He disliked 9.h4 d5, which had been seen in a game Li Chao-Borovikov in 2014.

9...♕e7 Here 9...0-0 might be the safest. I can't find anything better than 10.0-0, and now:

ANALYSIS DIAGRAM

– 10...♖e8 11.f4 exf3 12.♕xf3 cxd4 13.exd4 ♘xd4 14.♕f2 ♖xe5 15.♕xd4 d6 16.♗f4 ♗e6, when Black should be doing fine.

– 10...♕e7!? is also interesting. Shakh thought Black's position to be completely sound after 11.b3. For instance: 11...d6!? (after 11...♘xe5 12.dxe5 ♕xe5 13.♗b2 ♕e7 14.♕c2

♖e8 15.♖ad1 d6 16.♘b5 I would prefer White) 12.♘xc6 bxc6 13.♗b2 h5 14.g5 ♘h7 15.♘xe4 ♗xh3, and Black is fine.

10.b3!?

10...cxd4

In case of 10...♘b4!? (or 10...♘d8), Shakh had prepared a very nice idea: 11.a3 ♘a6 12.0-0 d6 13.f4!. Black doesn't really want to take the knight, as White gets a huge centre and very active pieces. It's a very unpleasant position, especially if your opponent has blitzed out all his moves so far.

ANALYSIS DIAGRAM

The play could continue 13...0-0 14.♖a2!? ♘c7 15.♖af2 dxe5! 16.fxe5 ♘h7 17.♘xe4 ♕h4! 18.♕e1 ♘e6 19.♖d2 ♕xe1 20.♖xe1, and the position is roughly equal.

After 10...♘xe5 11.dxe5 ♕xe5 12.♗b2 0-0 13.♕c2! (Maxime was afraid of 13.♖b1 ♕e7 14.h4 d6 15.g5 hxg5 16.hxg5 ♘h7 17.♖xh7!? ♔xh7 18.♘xe4) 13...♕e7 14.♘xe4 ♘xe4 15.♗xg7 ♔xg7 16.♕xe4 White has a stable edge.

11.exd4

11...♘xe5?!

The pawn is poisoned – Maxime had not seen White's 14th move.

11...0-0! was probably still sufficient to equalize, but some more precise moves are required: 12.0-0 ♘xe5 13.dxe5 ♕xe5 14.♗b2 d5 15.♕c1!? ♘h7! 16.cxd5 f5 17.♖b1 ♕d6! 18.♗a3 ♕e5 19.♗xf8 ♗xf8, and Black has good compensation on the dark squares for the exchange.

12.dxe5 ♕xe5 13.♗b2 d5 14.♕e2!

Maxime Vachier-Lagrave racks his brain over Mamedyarov's sharp opening idea. The Frenchman had a poor start, but bounced back in the second half.

After 17...♕d6 White goes 18.♖ad1 ♗d7 19.♕d2 and 20.♘xe4.
Maxime refrained from the endgame after 17...b6 18.♘xe4 ♘xe4 19.♗xg7 ♔xg7 20.♕xe4 ♕xe4 21.♖xe4 ♖xe4 22.♗xe4 ♗b7 23.♖c1 ♖d8 24.♖c7 ♗xd5 25.♗xd5 ♖xd5 26.♖xa7, when he is facing a very unpleasant defensive task and Black may be simply lost.
18.♘xe4 ♘xe4 19.♗xg7 ♔xg7 20.♕xe4 ♕xe4 21.♗xe4

21...h5?!
Instead of this pawn push, 21...♖ac8 is what Black should have done. However, White will play 22.d6 b6 23.♗b7!? ♖cd8 24.f4, when Black doesn't have any counterplay and will once again suffer.
22.gxh5 gxh5
MVL had missed that after 22...♖e5, White can simply take 23.hxg6 ♖ae8 (23...♖g5+ 24.♔h2 ♗xh3 25.♖g1 and White wins) 24.gxf7! ♔xf7 25.f3, with two extra pawns.
23.h4

Exploiting the weakness that Black has created in his camp with his 21st move.

Maxime had missed this smooth move. Now Black is in serious trouble. After 14.cxd5 0-0 Black would be doing absolutely OK.
14...♕e7 This leaves Black with no counterplay at all. Best was 14...d4, when White has a choice:

ANALYSIS DIAGRAM

– 15.♘b5 0-0 16.♗xd4 – Maxime thought this to be 'killing'. However, it's not so bad!: 16...♕e7! (16...♕f4 17.♕e3 is indeed killing) 17.0-0 ♗d7 18.♖fe1 ♗xb5 19.cxb5 ♖ad8 20.♖ad1 b6 21.♗xf6 ♗xf6 22.♕xe4 ♕xe4 23.♗xe4, with good drawing chances.
– 15.♘xe4!? 0-0 16.0-0-0 ♖d8 17.♘xf6+ ♕xf6 18.♖d3, and this looks excellent for White.
15.cxd5 0-0 16.0-0

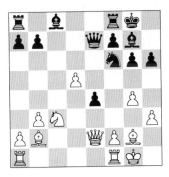

Now White will just be a clean pawn up.
16...♖e8 16...b6 17.♖fe1 ♗b7 18.♘xe4 ♘xe4 19.♗xg7 ♔xg7 20.♗xe4 ♖fd8 21.♕d2 is no better.
17.♖fe1 ♗d7

23...♖ac8 24.♗f3 ♖xe1+
25.♖xe1 ♔f6 26.d6 b6 27.♖e7
♖d8

Or 27...♗c6 28.♗e2 ♖g8+ 29.♔f1 a5
30.♗c4, with a winning advantage.

28.♗xh5 ♗e6 29.♖xa7 ♖xd6
30.♔g2 ♖d8 31.♗f3 ♔e5 32.♖a4

With two extra pawns it's a simple
technical win, so Maxime resigned.

Playing the World Champion

After my 0/3 start, I naturally didn't
expect a positive result for the
next game, since my opponent was
Magnus Carlsen. He had started with
a convincing 2½/3, including a very
nice Black victory against Maxime
Vachier-Lagrave. Nevertheless,
I felt quite confident and very motivated before the game. You don't get
the opportunity to play the World
Champion every day!

NOTES BY
Nico Georgiadis

Nico Georgiadis
Magnus Carlsen
Biel 2018 (4)
French Defence, Winawer Variation

1.e4 e6 A first surprise, but not really!
I was sure to get surprised within the
first five moves, I hadn't prepared too
much for this game anyway.
**2.d4 d5 3.♘c3 ♗b4 4.e5 c5 5.a3
♗a5!?**

Another surprise! I've hardly ever
had this line on the board in a classical game before. Carlsen went for
this so-called 'Armenian Variation'
in the hope of catching me flat-footed.
Luckily, I had just looked at this line in
detail about a month before the tournament, because my good friend GM

Paco Vallejo used it in several blitz
games against me and usually beat me
convincingly...
6.b4 cxd4 6...cxb4?! has been tried
a few times by Swiss IM Werner
Hug and some of his students. In the
meantime, the line has been basically
refuted, and people have completely
stopped playing it because of 7.♘b5
b3+ 8.c3.
7.♕g4 The critical move. The alternative 7.♘b5 would lead to a calmer
position in which White can fight for
a small, but stable edge.
7...♔f8!? This is a modern idea,
which was introduced in GM praxis
quite recently by GMs Edouard and
Vallejo. The old main line starts with
7...♘e7, but after 8.bxa5 dxc3 9.♕xg7
♖g8 10.♕xh7 White should be able to
maintain quite a large edge, as in, for
instance, Bacrot-Vaganian, Biel 2017.
8.♘b5 ♗c7?!

This move, which Carlsen played instantly, had been tried recently by Mamedyarov in a blitz game against Fedoseev. Nevertheless, it is an inferior move that should lead to an easy and pleasant advantage for White. I knew about the objective value of this move, so I was quite puzzled by Carlsen's opening choice. 8...♗b6 is the better move, which has been played by Edouard, Vallejo and others. Here, Black can at least fight for equality, even though, according to my analysis, he shouldn't quite reach it.

9.♕xd4!

9.♕g3 was played by Fedoseev in the above-mentioned blitz game. Even though White won that game convincingly, the text-move is even stronger.

9...♘c6

9...♘e7 is possible, in order to avoid the check on c5. However, White can simply play 10.♘xc7 ♕xc7 11.♘f3, and Black can't really capture the pawn on c2 due to his lack of development.

10.♕c5+ ♘ge7 11.♘xc7 ♕xc7 12.♘f3 b6

Up to here I remembered my analysis, but here my memory unfortunately let me down. I was convinced that the line I had looked at started with the move 13.♕d6 and that after a forced sequence of moves White ended up being clearly better.

This is why I tried for more than half an hour to make this move work. Even though I saw that after 13.♕d6 the position was anything but clear, I decided to give it a try after

spending so much time on it. That was probably the correct decision, since the other move, 13.♕c3, which I obviously saw, could/should have been played after two minutes.

13.♕d6?!

13.♕c3 was the move given in my analysis. After 13...d4 14.♕c4! (14.♘xd4?! ♕xe5+ 15.♘e2 ♗a6 is OK for Black) 14...♘g6 (after 14...♘d5 15.♗e2! White is better) 15.♗e2! ♕d7 16.♗b2, White has a very comfortable position.

13...♕xd6 14.exd6 ♘f5 15.♗f4 f6 16.g4!

16.♗b5 is useless after 16...♗b7.

16...♘fd4 17.♘xd4 ♘xd4 18.0-0-0 e5

19.♖xd4!? Objectively not entirely correct, but that was the idea behind my 13th move.

In the post-mortem, Carlsen correctly mentioned 19.h3!, which could possibly delay the exchange sacrifice. On the other hand, it allows 19...♘e6!? 20.♗g3 ♗b7 21.♗g2 ♔e8!, and the position seems to be a touch more pleasant for Black.

19...exd4 20.♗b5 ♗xg4!

Fearless and strong. During the

game, I had expected 20...♗e6, when White could continue with either 21.♖d1 or 21.♖e1!? ♔f7 22.♗d7.

21.♖e1 g5 22.♗g3

22...♖d8! I had missed this move in my calculations. I had only seen 22...h5 23.d7 ♔f7 24.♖e8! (24.♗d6 ♗e6!) 24...♖axe8 25.dxe8♕+ ♖xe8 26.♗xe8+ ♔xe8, when a draw would be the likely outcome.

23.♖e7 h5

24.h4?!

24.f4 was far stronger and would have given White very interesting compensation for the exchange: 24...h4 (24...♖xd6 25.♖e8+ ♔g7 26.♖e7=) 25.♗f2 ♗f5! (25...♖xd6 26.♖xa7, and despite being and exchange and a pawn down, White has excellent compensation due to his active pieces and the outstanding dark-squared bishop) 26.♗xd4 ♖xd6 27.♖e8+ ♔g7 28.♖xh8 ♔xh8 29.fxg5 ♔h7 30.gxf6 ♖d8 31.a4!, and with accurate play White should hold.

24...gxh4 25.♗f4

25.♗xh4 ♖xd6 26.♖xa7 ♖g8 seemed hopeless to me during the game.

25...♗f5

25...a5! was probably the easiest way for Black to obtain a large advantage, as Carlsen correctly pointed out after

the game: 26.♗c6 axb4 27.axb4 ♗f5 28.♖b7 ♖h7 29.♖xb6 ♗g7 30.♗xd5 ♖g4 31.♗h2 d3!? 32.cxd3 ♖d4, and Black's position looks close to winning.

26.♖xa7

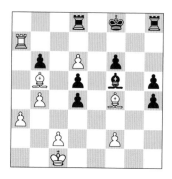

26...♖h7

We both disregarded 26...♖c8!, which would have given Black a better version than in the game after 27.♖c7 (27.d7? ♖xc2+ 28.♔d1 ♔e7, winning) 27...♖xc7 28.dxc7 ♔e7 29.a4 ♖g8, since Black can activate his rook immediately: 30.a5 bxa5 31.bxa5 d3! 32.c3 (after 32.cxd3? ♗d7 Black wins) 32...♖g1+ 33.♔d2 (33.♔b2 ♖b1+!, and Black wins) 33...♖a1 34.♗xd3 ♖a2+! 35.♔c1 ♗e6 36.a6 ♔d7, and according to the engine, Black has a winning advantage, although there is still some work to be done.

27.♖c7

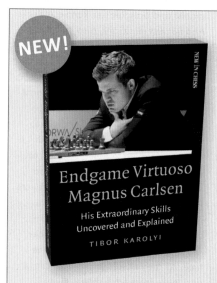

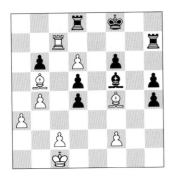

27...♗d7?! Now Black loses almost his entire advantage. Carlsen had simply missed my next move. Logical would have been 27...♔g8!, with the idea of ...♖g7 and good winning chances. Nevertheless, the position is still far from trivial, and with a perfect defence White might even be able to hold. E.g.: 28.♗c6! ♖g7 29.a4 ♖g1+ 30.♔d2 h3 31.♗xd5+ ♔h8, and now:

ANALYSIS DIAGRAM

A) 32.a5 bxa5 33.bxa5 ♖f1! (but not 33...♖a1 34.♖c5 ♔g7?!, because of 35.a6! ♖xa6 36.♗c4 ♖a4 37.♗b3, with a draw) 34.♔e2 ♖a1 35.♖c5 ♔g7 36.a6 ♖xa6 37.♗c4 ♖a4 38.♗b3 d3+!, and Black wins.

B) 32.♖f7!? ♖c8! 33.♖c7 ♖f1! 34.♔e2 ♖b1 35.♗e4! ♗g4+ 36.♗f3

ANALYSIS DIAGRAM

Magnus Carlsen has every reason to scratch his head. After a flashy start, the draw against Nico Georgiadis proved to be a turning point for the World Champion.

and here Black has two options:

B1) 36...♖xc7 37.♗xg4! (37.dxc7 ♗c8 and wins) 37...♖xc2+ 38.♔d3 ♖c3+ 39.♔e4 ♖e1+ 40.♔xd4 ♖cc1 41.♔d3!!, and according to the engines, White can hold.

B2) 36...♖d8 37.♗xg4 hxg4 38.♔e7 d3+! 39.♔xd3 ♖xd6+! (after 39...♖xb4 40.♗g3 the strong passer on d6 secures White sufficient counterplay) 40.♗xd6 ♖d1+ 41.♔e4 (41.♔c4 ♖xd6, and wins) 41...♖e1+! 42.♔f4 ♖xe7 43.♔xg4 ♖h7 44.♗h2 ♖a7 45.a5! bxa5 46.bxa5 ♖xa5 47.♔xh3, and this position is a draw: 47...♖c5 48.f3 ♖xc2 49.♗f4 ♔g7 50.♔g4, with a fortress.

28.♗c6! h3 29.♔d2

29...♖g7?! Based on an oversight by Carlsen. This leads to a forced draw.

A better try was 29...♔e8 30.♗xd5 ♖g7 31.♔d3 ♖g4 32.♗h2 b5!, and the engine likes Black here, as he always has the idea of giving back the exchange with ...♖g2. However, I don't think that in a practical game Black is so much better here.

30.♗h6 ♗xc6

30...h2? 31.♗xd5 and White wins, because Black finds himself in zugzwang.

31.♖xg7 ♖xd6

32.♖g5+!

Fortunately, I managed to find this strong move despite being low on time already.

After 32.♖g3+?! ♔f7 33.♖xh3 ♔g6 34.♗f4 ♔e6, Black keeps an extra pawn and serious winning chances.

32...♔f7

32...♔e7 33.♖xh5 ♗d7 34.♗f4 ♖c6 35.♖h7+! is what Carlsen had overlooked (after 35.♖xd5?! ♖c4 Black is pressing): 35...♔e8 36.♖h8+ ♔f7 37.♖h7+, and Black can't escape the perpetual check without giving up the h3-pawn.

33.♖xh5 ♗b5

33...♗d7 34.♗f4 ♖c6 35.♖h7+ (or even 35.♖xd5), with a draw.

34.♖xh3 ♖e6 35.♖f3

35...♔g6

At this point 35...♖e5!? was an interesting try, but White could even give up the f2-pawn by playing 36.♖g3!? ♖e2+ 37.♔c1 ♖xf2 38.♖g7+ ♔e8 39.♖g4 d3 40.cxd3 ♗xd3 41.♖f4, with a draw.

36.♗f4 ♖c6 37.♗g3 ♖c4 38.♖d3 ♔f5 39.♖f3+ ♔e6 40.♖d3 f5 41.f3 f4 42.♗f2

42.♗xf4 ♗a4 43.♔e1 ♗xc2 44.♖d2 d3 45.♗g3 ♖c8 could still be troublesome for White, even though his position is objectively fine.

42...♔e5 43.c3

At this point, I was expecting the scoresheets to be signed within minutes.

43...♖c6!

Very strong! Carlsen still finds a way to make me suffer a bit longer.

43...dxc3+ 44.♖xc3 d4 45.♖xc4 ♗xc4 46.a4, and the draw would be official.

44.♖xd4 ♖h6 45.♔c1

45.♔e1?! is less precise, due to 45...♖h1+ 46.♔d2 ♖h3.

45...♖h3 46.♖d2 ♖xf3

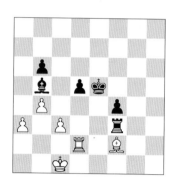

47.♗d4+!

I guess that after 47.♔b2 Carlsen wanted to try 47...♖xf2!? 48.♖xf2 ♔e4, and White already has to defend accurately: 49.a4! ♗xa4 50.♖e2+! ♔d3 51.♖e5 f3 52.♖xd5+ ♔e3 53.♖d6 f2 54.♖e6+ ♔d2 55.♖f6, with a draw.

47...♔e4 48.♔b2 ♖d3 49.♖xd3

49.♖e2+ ♖e3 50.♖d2 was also sufficient, but the text-move just ends the game.

49...♔xd3 50.♗xb6 ♗a4 51.♗a7 f3 52.♗g1 ♔d2 53.♗a7 ♗d1 54.♗c5 ♗a4 55.♗a7 ♔e2 56.c4!

56...d4

Or 56...dxc4 57.♔c3 ♗b5 58.a4 ♗xa4 59.♔xc4, with a draw.

57.♗xd4 ♔d3 58.♗a7 ♔xc4

Draw.

A veritable thriller, with several ups and downs! Needless to say that after my bad start I was very pleased with a draw against the World Champion! And even though I lost the next three games, this draw helped me a lot psychologically, because the worst case scenario of scoring 0/10 was no longer possible!

Under pressure

Unfortunately, I was a bit too optimistic after the game against Carlsen, which was one of the reasons why in the next game I entered a very sharp line with Black, which I had never played before, against Maxime Vachier-Lagrave. In retrospect, I regret that choice, but one is always smarter afterwards! He surprised me with a rare move, and I couldn't recall my analysis. I was under pressure, blundered a pawn and lost the game. Then I lost to Mamedyarov with white in the Najdorf. I was surprised by that opening choice and didn't look at it before the game. After the opening I was once again under pressure and after missing one chance to equalize I collapsed in time-trouble and lost that game as well.

That same round saw the following tense encounter. Following his disastrous ½/3 start Maxime Vachier-Lagrave made an impressive comeback and eventually finished on a decent +1.

NOTES BY
Nico Georgiadis

Peter Svidler
Maxime Vachier-Lagrave
Biel 2018 (6)
English Opening, Symmetrical Variation

1.c4 c5 2.♘f3 ♘f6 3.♘c3 d5 4.cxd5 ♘xd5 5.e4 ♘b4 6.♗c4 ♘d3+ 7.♔e2 ♘f4+ 8.♔f1 ♘e6 The main move here and MVL's favourite. The alternative, 8...♘d3, has been played by, amongst others, Peter Svidler.

9.d3 Quite a rare move. Svidler tried 9.h4 twice in last year's World Cup encounter against the same opponent. MVL seemed to be well prepared, at least in the second game, and after 9...♘d4 10.d3 e6!? (10...♘bc6 11.♘b5!? gave White some pressure in the first game, which eventually ended in a draw) 11.♗f4 a6 12.♘xd4 cxd4 13.♘e2 ♘c6 14.a3 ♗d6, Black comfortably equalized and later went on to win.
However, MVL hasn't faced 9.b4 yet, which is actually the main move.

9...♘c6 9...♘d4? would be a major blunder due to 10.♗f4, followed by ♘d5.

10.h4

10...g6?! This should accommodate White. The best response seems to be 10...h5, as the g5-square is still controlled by Black's knight on e6: 11.♘g5 g6 12.♘xe6 ♗xe6 13.♗xe6 fxe6 14.♗e3 ♗g7 15.♗xc5 0-0, with a double-edged position.

11.h5 ♗g7

12.♗e3 12.♕d2!? was the interesting move Maxime proposed after the game. After the sample line 12...♗d7 13.hxg6 fxg6! (13...hxg6? 14.♖xh8+ ♗xh8 15.♕h6! was White's malicious idea) 14.♘d5 ♘cd4 15.♘xd4 ♗xd4 16.a4 White's position seems preferable to me.
12.♘d5!? was another good move, after which it's hard to come up with a satisfactory plan for Black.
Peter rejected the immediate 12.h6 because of 12...♗d4!? (however, even here Black could go simply 12...♗f6!? 13.♘d5 0-0 14.♘xf6+ exf6, and his position wouldn't be too bad).

12...♘ed4

13.h6?! White could claim a very pleasant advantage after 13.♖c1!? ♘xf3 14.♕xf3 ♘e5 15.♕e2 ♘xc4 16.dxc4 ♗xc3 17.♖xc3 ♕c7 18.hxg6 fxg6 19.♖d3.

13...♗f6 14.♘d5 ♗g4 15.♘xf6+ exf6 16.♗xd4 16.♕a4 ♗xf3 17.gxf3 0-0, and Black's active knights compensate for White's bishop pair.

16...♘xd4 After 16...♗xf3?! Peter had prepared a nice trap: 17.♗xf7+! ♔xf7 18.♕b3+ ♔e8 19.♕e6+! ♕e7 20.♕xe7+ ♘xe7 21.♗xf6 ♖f8 22.♗xe7 ♔xe7 23.gxf3 ♖xf3 24.♔e2 ♖af8 25.♖af1, with an extra pawn and good winning chances.

17.♕a4+

17...♕d7!? The safest move, forcing the queen swap. Black had a bunch of other options:

17...♔e7 18.♕a3! (18.♘xd4 ♕xd4 19.♕b3 b5! – a strong move that both had missed. After any other move he'd be worse. Here, it's White who must be careful) 18...♖c8 19.♘xd4 ♕xd4, with an unclear position.

Interesting was 17...♘c6!? 18.♗d5 0-0 19.♗xc6 ♕xd3+ 20.♔g1 bxc6 21.♕xc6 ♕d8! 22.♕xc5 ♖e8, when Black should definitely have some compensation for the pawn.

Finally, after 17...♗d7?! 18.♕a3 ♕e7 (18...b5?! won't work because of 19.♗d5!) 19.♘xd4 cxd4 20.♕b3 White manages to keep the queens

on the board, which Maxime wanted to avoid.

18.♕xd7+ ♗xd7 19.♘xd4 cxd4

20.e5? This move is unnecessary and only gives Black chances, as Svidler pointed out after the game. With the very natural move 20.♔e2, White would basically not run any risk. But it has to be said that Black is not having any serious problems either, so a draw would be the logical outcome. For instance, 20...♔e7 21.♖hc1 ♖hc8 22.a4 (22.♗d5 ♗e6!?) 22...f5, and Black will probably hold. Nevertheless, I'd definitely pick White here due to the advanced pawn on h6, on which Black must always keep an eye.

20...fxe5 21.♖e1 f6 22.f4 ♖f8 Also 22...b5!? 23.♗d5 ♖c8 24.fxe5 ♔e7 looks dangerous for White, since the black rook will penetrate on the c-file.

23.♔g1 ♔e7 24.fxe5 f5 25.♖h4 f4! Peter had expected something like 25...♗c6? 26.♖xd4 ♖ad8, when White is clearly better.

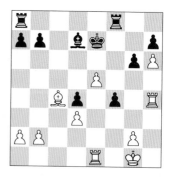

26.♖e4? After having missed Black's 27th move at an earlier stage, Peter still tried to make this line work and calculated a forced sequence in which he saw himself surviving. Unfortunately, there was a hole in that line, too. Instead of this, White could have chosen the safer option 26.♗d5! ♖ac8 (26...g5?! 27.♖h5

Peter Svidler suffered a disappointing loss against MVL, but otherwise the Russian had a solid performance and finished on +1.

'After Maxime had opened the score, Magnus kept scoring in Arjen Robben style and our team soon had to admit defeat.'

♖f5 28.♗e4 ♖xe5 29.♖xg5! ♖xg5 30.♗xb7+, with an extra pawn for White) 27.♗xb7 ♖b8 28.♗e4 ♖xb2 29.♖f1 g5 30.♖h5, and White is OK.

26...g5 27.♖h5 ♖f5!
A very important move.

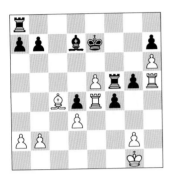

28.g4?! This was the idea, but it loses on the spot. Anyway, White's position was already difficult. The engine defends with 28.♔f2 ♗c6 29.♖xd4 ♖xe5 30.♗b3!, when Black is obviously much better, but White can still hold on for a while. For instance, after 30...♖f8 31.♗d1!, stopping f3. 28.e6?! was no better: 28...♗e8 29.♖h3 ♖d8, and Black's position is overwhelming.

28...fxg3 29.♖g4 ♖af8!

30.♖hxg5 After 30.♖gxg5 ♖f1+ 31.♔g2 we'd get to 31...♖1f2+!, the move that wasn't on Peter's radar. Now White can't escape the mating net: 32.♔g1 (32.♔xg3 ♖8f3+ 33.♔h4 ♖h3 mate) 32...♗c6 33.♖g7+ ♔e8, and mate is coming.

Another mate is seen after 30.♖xg3 ♗c6 31.♖gxg5 ♖f1+ 32.♔h2 ♖8f2+ 33.♔h3 ♖h1+ 34.♔g4 ♖g2+ 35.♔f4 ♖f1 mate.

30...♖f1+ 31.♔g2 ♗c6+

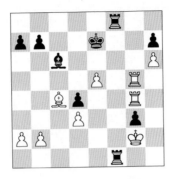

And White resigned in view of 32.♔xg3 ♖8f3+ (the most straight-forward, but 32...♖g1+ wins as well) 33.♔h2 ♖3f2+ 34.♔h3 (34.♖g2 is the only way to avoid mate) 34...♖h1+ 35.♔g3 ♖g2+ 36.♔f4 ♖f1 mate.

A very disappointing game for Peter Svidler, since he had got a pleasant position in which he could hope to press in a long game; but he suddenly found himself on the other side of the fence after messing up the position with 20.e5?.

A glimpse of hope

After Round 6 the players had a well-needed rest day. The night before the rest day there was a football match, and of course I didn't miss the opportunity to take part. I had a glimpse of hope that at least I would beat them in football. As if! After Maxime had opened the score for the opposition, Magnus kept scoring in Arjen Robben style and our team soon had to admit defeat. Nevertheless, we had great fun and it was a good diversion to moving wooden pieces on a square board.

After a boat trip on the rest day I prepared a lot (maybe too much) for my next game against Peter Svidler. I expected him to play some Sicilian and was armed to the teeth against all of them. I surprised him with a sharp line in the Najdorf, but then he played one move that I had forgotten to look at, even though I had wanted

to do so the previous evening. I was very upset with myself during the game and trying to figure out how one can be so oblivious. Unfortunately, during a chess game you don't have time to solve such philosophical questions. As the game went on, I soon sacrificed material when there was absolutely no need to do so. After that Peter showed excellent defensive skills and the game was decided.

After such a pitiful loss all I felt was frustration. This frustration had to be flushed away with some beers and a game of cards in the evening. After that I was ready for a big fight against David Navara. In an interesting battle I was worse after the opening but fought back until we reached the following position. As usual, I had only 15 minutes remaining on the clock, with 14 moves to go.

David Navara
Nico Georgiadis
Biel 2018 (8)

position after 26.♗xa7

26...♖a8!?
26...♕d6! was even stronger: 27.♗xe4 (if 27.♕b3 ♘d2 28.♕xb6 ♕xb6 29.♗xb6 ♘xf1 wins the exchange, with good winning chances for Black) 27...dxe4 28.♕b3+ ♗d5 29.♕xb6 ♕d7, and the bishop on a7 is lost.
27.♕b3 ♕f7!

A relaxed David Navara during the boat trip on the free day.
The Czech GM was not in his best shape, but kept fighting till the very end.

That was the idea. Now White has to take a difficult decision.

28.♕xb6?! David played this move quite quickly, intending to put me under pressure as much as possible. However, better was 28.♖f4! ♘d2 29.♖xe8+ ♕xe8 30.♕c3 ♕e3+ 31.♖f2, and White survives.
28...♖e6 29.♕a5 ♗c6

30.♖xe4!? A gamble, hoping for mistakes in time-trouble. After the obvious 30.♗xe4 dxe4 31.d5 ♖e5 32.♕c5 ♕xd5 33.♕xd5+ ♖xd5 34.♗f2 ♖xa2 Black is probably winning. An important detail is that 35.♖xe4 fails to 35...♕g5.
30...dxe4 31.♗c4 ♖xa7 32.♕c5

The key position: Black is a rook up, but he has to defend against the threats 33.♗xe6 and 34.♕xa7. There were two adequate solutions, after which resignation would have been White's only option. Regrettably, I was unable to find either of them.
32...♖c7?
The simplest was 32...♖d7!. All you need to see is that after 33.d5, 33...♕h5! finishes the game in one move: 34.dxe6 ♕xc5+.

32...♖a4! was also strong. Black will remain a piece up after 33.♗b3 ♖a6 34.♗c4 (34.d5 ♖e5, and game over) 34...♗b7.
33.♖c1! e3

34.b4!?
An unbelievably brave decision, intending to play for a win. Objectively, the move is just bad, but with 30 seconds left on my clock, I could easily blunder. At the press conference, David said that he didn't care about the objective value; he just wanted to win the game, and felt this was a good chance. Impressive!
Both 34.♗xe6!? ♕xe6 35.d5 ♕e4 36.dxc6 e2 37.♕c3 (37.♔f2? ♖xc6! 38.♕xc6 e1♕+ was a nice trick that I had seen during the game) 37...♖xc6 38.♕b3+ ♔f8 39.♕b8+ ♔f7 40.♕b3+ and 34.d5!? ♗xd5 35.♕xd5 ♔h8 36.♖e1 ♖xc4 37.♕xc4 ♕d7 would have led to an approximately equal position.
34...e2 35.♖e1

35...♔h8
35...♖c8!, with the idea of 36.♖xe2 ♗d7!, is very strong and would once again have won the game.
35...♗b7?? was a move I considered,

but this one would have given the point to White!: 36.♗xe6 ♛xe6 37.♛xc7 ♛e3+ 38.♔h1 ♛f2 39.♛b8+!, and White wins.

36.b5

36.♖xe2 ♖ce7 37.♖xe6 ♖xe6 38.♛xc6 ♖xc6 39.♗xf7 ♖b6 40.a3 ♖a6 looks good for Black, but apparently White holds with 41.b5 ♖xa3 42.♗d5 g6 43.b6 ♖a1+ 44.♔f2 ♖b1 45.b7 ♔g7 46.♔e3 ♔f8 47.♗e4, when the strong passer on b7 guarantees White sufficient counterplay.

36...♛e7?! After this, White can liquidate to a draw. With 30 seconds on the clock, I had missed that after 36...♗xb5 37.♛xb5 Black can unpin with 37...♛e8!, when he is still winning.

37.♗xe6 ♛xc5 38.dxc5 ♗xb5 39.♗g4 ♖xc5 40.♗xe2 ♗a4 41.♖b1 g6 42.♖b4 ♖c2 43.♗d1 ♖c1 44.♖xa4 ♖xd1+ 45.♔f2 ♖d2+ 46.♔f3 ♔g7 47.♖a7+ ♔h6 48.a4 ♖a2 49.a5 ♔g5 50.a6 h5 51.♖a8 ♔f5 52.h4

And a draw was agreed.

Despite the time-trouble excuse, this was clearly another setback,

'Many people expected a miracle from the World Champion, and I am sure Carlsen expected one from himself as well.'

not winning this position with an extra rook, although, as mentioned above, my approach didn't allow me to resign two rounds before the end, because two more chances against world-class players were awaiting me! At least, for the first time in the event, I had been close to winning a game.

The clash of the titans
The game against MVL in Round 9 was the least interesting one. He chose a very solid opening and we quickly reached an endgame that I thought I couldn't possibly lose. Maxime pressed regardless, but with some precise moves I managed to hold without too many problems.

Much more exciting was the clash of the titans between tournament leader Shakhriyar Mamedyarov and Magnus Carlsen! The World Champion had to win to retain chances to finish first. Here it is, annotated by Anish Giri.

NOTES BY
Anish Giri

Shakhriyar Mamedyarov
Magnus Carlsen
Biel 2018 (9)
King's Indian, Yugoslav System

As he was trailing Shakh Mamedyarov by a full point, many people expected a miracle from the World Champion, and I am sure Carlsen expected one from himself as well.
1.d4 ♘f6 2.c4 g6 3.g3 ♗g7 4.♗g2 0-0 5.♘c3 d6 6.♘f3 c5 7.0-0 ♘c6
I once played this system myself, in fact, just like Magnus, with the intention of getting a double-edged game. The beautiful thing about the

g3 system against the King's Indian, however, is that Black can't have both equality and winning chances. In this game, Magnus decides to go for the former, hoping that the latter will arise out of nothing, as so often happens.

8.e3!? A bit strange, but still a creative way to enter somewhat unchartered territory. Black is spoilt for choice here, since he can choose from many semi-waiting moves. Carlsen, however, decides to solve his problems radically.
8.dxc5 dxc5 9.♗e3 would be my choice if I was looking to shut down the game. This was what Wang Yue did against me. My deep preparation, following an old Kasparov game, gave me comfortable play, but I failed to crack the most solid of the Chinese players.
8...d5

I read that Magnus claimed afterwards that with the pawn on e3

instead of e2, 'White has to look for equality'.

It sounds like a strange claim and a rare case of the World Champion being wrong, given his incredible opening culture and almost unmatched feel for opening subtleties and nuances, but if we think a little more deeply and realize that Magnus considered this game a must-win and Shakh a must-draw, this evaluation becomes a lot more understandable. Given his psychological disposition, the player looking for blood often starts considering any slightly unbalanced position to be in his favour and subconsciously focuses on the lines in which his opponent tries to maintain the clarity and keep the symmetry.

To get back to the chessboard, I imagine Magnus referred to exchanges on d5, followed by ♘e5xc6, when it's true that Black is doing very well.

9.cxd5

9.dxc5!? dxc4 10.♕a4 is also testing, but Black seems to be doing alright in a sample line that I had sketched out here: 10...♗e6 11.♘g5 ♗g4!? 12.♕xc4 ♘e5 13.♕b5!? (setting up a small tactic) 13...h6 14.c6!? (suddenly attacking the e5-knight) 14...♘xc6 15.♕xb7 ♗d7 16.♘f3 ♖b8 17.♕a6 ♕c8!, with excellent compensation for the pawn thanks to the nice open b-file and the pressure along the a1-h8 diagonal, both targeting the extra b2-pawn.

9...♘xd5 10.♘xd5 ♕xd5 11.♘e5

11...♕d6

11...♕d8 would avoid the sequence in the game, but here it becomes more attractive for White to simplify:

12.♘xc6 bxc6 13.dxc5 ♕xd1 14.♖xd1 ♗e6, when Black should have enough compensation for the pawn to keep the balance, while Vachier-Lagrave, a big fan of pawn sacrifices in the Grünfeld, would probably already think he was winning.

12.♘c4

Daring to accept the challenge. Obviously, White trying to force a draw here would be what Black was counting on.

12...♕c7 13.d5 ♖d8 14.♗d2 ♘b4?!

Again, following the subconscious 'any imbalance is good for me' rule. Typically, in a must-win game, the sense of danger is dimmed and I imagine Magnus sort of overlooked the ♘xf7 sac in the 15. e4 variation.

14...♘e5 15.♘xe5 ♗xe5 would lead to equality. Black will follow up with ...e6, and I don't think White is in time to really get anything going here.

15.♗xb4?! A moment of silence for White's dark squares.

However, 15.e4! was natural, and with natural moves one must try really hard to make them work, because as a rule, the natural ones are the good ones: 15...b5 16.♗f4 ♕b7 (16...e5 is met by 17.d6!, when Black has nothing better than 17...♕c6 18.♘xe5 ♕xd6 19.♕xd6

♖xd6, and now he gets a cheapo: 20.♘xf7!) 17.♘e5 g5.

ANALYSIS DIAGRAM

This indeed looks like a problem, but: 18.♘xf7! ♔xf7 19.♗xg5, and it appears that the black queen on b7 is the culprit here, since a3, throwing away the active knight, is on the agenda and the main issue for Black is the h1-a8 diagonal, meaning that tricks with d6 and e5 are in the air.

15...cxb4 16.♖c1

16...a5!? Ambitious and also strong. It was also possible to play more modestly with 16...♗d7 and never ever lose this game, but the move in the game is better.

17.a3 bxa3 18.bxa3 a4!

Fixing the pawn on a3, and now, if Black follows this up with ...b5, he

Biel 2018				1	2	3	4	5	6		TPR
1 Shakhriyar Mamedyarov	IGM	AZE	2801	**	½ 1	1 ½	½ ½	½ 1	1 1	7½	2921
2 Magnus Carlsen	IGM	NOR	2842	½ 0	**	1 ½	½ ½	1 ½	½ 1	6	2792
3 Maxime Vachier-Lagrave	IGM	FRA	2779	0 ½	0 ½	**	½ 1	½ 1	1 ½	5½	2768
4 Peter Svidler	IGM	RUS	2753	½ ½	½ ½	½ 0	**	½ ½	1 1	5½	2773
5 David Navara	IGM	CZE	2741	½ 0	0 ½	½ 0	½ ½	**	1 ½	4	2668
6 Nico Georgiadis	IGM	SUI	2526	0 0	½ 0	0 ½	0 0	0 ½	**	1½	2487

cat. XX

will be the one having all the fun.
19.♕d3

19...♗f5? Way too ambitious. Obviously, it would be positionally desirable if Black kept control of the e5-square, but this totally backfires in view of 21.♕e3!.
19...♖b8! was anyway stronger, threatening ...b5, when it's White's job to think of what he is going to come up with to create any sort of counterplay. In this sense, giving White e4 for free is once again completely wrong.
20.e4 ♗d7 21.♕e3!

Now White completely takes over the initiative, but Black is still in the game, obviously.
21...♖a6 22.e5! b5 23.d6

The clash of the titans. Magnus Carlsen got no chance to play for a win against Shakhriyar Mamedyarov and even lost when, in a precarious position, he made a horrible blunder.

23...♕b8 Keeping the queens on is still okay, but two moves later, in a critical position, Black makes a major mistake, so in hindsight it was better to have gone for an endgame at once.
With accurate play, 23...♕a7 would have led to an equal endgame: 24.dxe7 ♖e8 25.♕xa7 ♖xa7 26.♘d6 ♖xe7 27.f4 ♗f8! 28.♗d5. White keeps a much more active position, but with long-term trumps on the queenside Black will undoubtedly draw this after some good moves.
24.dxe7 ♖e8 25.♖fd1 ♖xe7 26.♕c5

26...♕f8?
26...♗f8! would have maintained the balance: 27.♘d6 ♗e6 (27...♖e8 28.♗d5

♗xd6 29.exd6 ♖c8 allows White some attractive options, 30.♕c7!? or 30.♗xf7!?, but both of them only yield equality at the end of the complications) 28.♗d5 ♖e8! 29.♕xb5 ♕xb5 30.♘xb5 ♗xd5 31.♖xd5 ♖a5, and the weak a3-pawn will secure Black enough counterplay to escape.
27.♘e3!
The move Black had missed. Now the e5-pawn can't be captured and White has many ideas of his own, 28.♗b7 being the most obvious threat.
27...♗e6 Giving up the b5-pawn seems like the best option after the unfortunate mistake on the previous move.
28.♕xb5 ♖aa7 29.♘d5

29...♗xd5

This is just going to be sad, but such is life for Black at this point.

29...♖ed7 30.♘f6+ ♗xf6 31.exf6 looks extremely dangerous for Black. The extra f6-pawn is a little weak, but there are no guarantees that it will be captured, and for now the black king is in a mating net and is likely to have some back rank issues as well.

30.♖xd5 ♖eb7 31.♕d3 ♖b8 32.h4 ♕e8 33.♕d4 ♕e7

34.f4? It was more flexible to start with 34.♔h2, which is also a lot more pleasing optically, besides being a much better move, according to the computer.

34...♗f8 35.♔h2 ♖ab7

35...♖c7 appears to be a better defence: 36.♖xc7 ♕xc7 37.♖d7 ♕c2 38.♕d5 ♕f5, but it is hard to be sure that nothing bad will happen to the f7-pawn.

36.♕xa4?! Given the tournament situation, Shakh finally decides to just go with a very promising endgame, despite the drawish tendencies.

36.♖d6! would apparently be winning: 36...♖b2 37.♔h3!, and Black has no way to exploit the fact that the f8-bishop almost attacks the d6-rook, since 37...♕e8 can be met by 38.♗c6; if not, 38.♗d5 is coming and the f7-pawn's days are numbered.

36...♕xa3 37.♕xa3 ♗xa3 38.♖cd1 ♗e7 39.♔h3

39...♖c7

Not only in rook endings, the general rule is often to place the pawn on h5. After 39...h5, however, White's light-square dominance could turn out fatal if White blasts open the kingside pawn structure with 40.f5!.

40.h5 gxh5!?

Utter desperation, but Black actually manages to hold the last line of defence this way.

41.f5 f6 42.e6

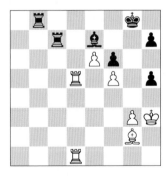

42...♖b3!

This is brilliant. It was tempting to assume that Black has to stay with the king on f8, but then it quickly becomes clear that the h7-pawn will eventually fall, because Black has two weak points in his position, e7 and h7, which are just a little too far apart for him to hold. This set-up of doubling the rooks on the c-file, bringing the king to h6 and potentially creating some counterplay against the g3-pawn as well, is extremely elegant, and it was only the fact that this was really not Carlsen's day, that stopped him from holding this endgame.

After 42...♔f8, 43.♗f3 would be a good start, picking up the h5-pawn and clearing the h-file for the potential h7-pawn hunt.

43.♖d7 ♖bc3 44.♖a1 ♔g7! 45.♖a8 ♔h6!

The king is excellently hidden here.

46.♖e8 ♗b4 47.♖b8 ♗e7 48.♗e4 Allowing a tactical opportunity that Black understandably missed or decided not to go for.

48...♖3c4

Black should also be able to hold passively, so this should be OK as well.

After 48...♖e3!? 49.♖xc7 ♗d6 White's best bet is winning the exchange: 50.♖g8 ♗xc7 51.e7 ♖xe4 52.e8♕ ♖xe8 53.♖xe8, but after further simplifications we get a drawn endgame: 53...♔g5 54.♖e7 ♗e5 55.♖xh7 ♗d6 56.♖h8 ♗e5 57.♖g8+ ♔xf5 58.♔h4 ♗e6 59.♖h8 f5 60.♖xh5 ♗f6+ 61.♔h3 ♗e5, with a draw, as confirmed by the tablebases.

49.♗d5 ♖4c5 50.♗e4 ♖c4

'A fascinating struggle that proves that in a situation as tense as the one on that day in Biel, even the gods are human.'

51.♗d5 ♖4c5 52.♖b7 ♖xd7 53.♖xd7

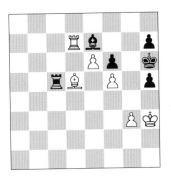

53...♖a5? Nobody likes defending and it is never easy, but I am sure that in the right mood and with a good energy level, a player of Magnus's calibre would not be this sloppy. 53...♗f8! just avoids any rook endings. Just in case, even if they weren't winning: 54.♖f7 ♗d6!.

54.♗c6?

With 54.♗c4! White should have forced the black rook to a bad square and gone for the rook ending: 54...♖a4 55.♗d3! ♖a3 56.♖xe7 ♖xd3 57.♖e8 ♖e3 58.♖g8 ♖e1 59.♔g2 ♖e5. Now the only way to make progress is: 60.g4! hxg4 61.♔g3, but this does win: 61...♖e1 (61...♔h5 62.♖xg4 ♖xf5 loses to 63.♖e4 ♖g5+ 64.♔f4 ♖g8 65.♔f5) 62.♖xg4

ANALYSIS DIAGRAM

This is just slowly losing. Black can't do anything, and given the cut-off

king, the protected thorn on e6 is too much: 62...♖e5 63.♖g8 ♖e1 64.♔f3 ♖e5 65.♔f4 ♖e1 66.♖g3, and White wins.

54...♗a3! 55.♖f7 ♖e5! 56.♔h4

From the press conference transcript that I read it seems that Black believed he was lost at this point, which obviously doesn't help. But still, as a chess professional I am sure that Carlsen hated himself for the next move.

56...♗c1??

56...♗b4 even seems to hold the draw, but losing in one move due to a blunder is incredibly painful and unpleasant regardless. After 56...♗b4 the play could have continued 57.♗f3 (57.♖xf6+ ♔g7 58.♖f7+ ♔h6 59.g4 ♗e1+ 60.♔h3 ♖e3+ 61.♔g2, and both 61...♗h4 and 61...♗b4 would hold the pawns, and the maximum White can get out of his passed pawns is a rook and bishop vs rook ending) 57...♗d2! 58.♖xf6+ ♔g7 59.♖f7+ ♔h6. Black seems to hold and the piece sac 60.♗xh5 doesn't change that assessment: 60...♗g5+ 61.♔h3 ♔xh5 62.♖xh7+ ♗h6.

57.e7

Black resigned.

A fascinating struggle that proves that in a situation as tense as the one on that day in Biel, even the gods are human.

■ ■ ■

With this win, Shakhriyar Mamedyarov sealed his tournament victory. The Azeri number one described his play after the tournament in an interview with Teimour Tushiev: 'I used to play more aggressively, while now you might say I play more wisely'. His play wasn't particularly aggressive, he just played practical and sound moves, which is an unpleasant combination for any opponent.

Also, his opening preparation was excellent as usual. Interesting opening ideas formed the basis of his quick victories. And he was extremely consistent. As far as I can see, he was in danger of losing only once, against Navara in Round 2, which is remarkable against such opposition. Since he survived in that game, too, he was the only player who finished the tournament unbeaten. Mamedyarov dominated the tournament and the final standings are evidence of his domination.

Only human

Mamedyarov's main rival, Magnus Carlsen, had to settle for second place. The World Champion was clearly not at his best, especially in the second half. Except for his smooth victory against Vachier-Lagrave and his swashbuckling draw in Round 3 against Peter Svidler, his play couldn't convince me, and I'm sure he was quite disappointed about it, too. Bearing in mind that his ability to sense any kind of danger is normally outstanding, it was remarkable that in several games he overlooked moves that didn't seem all that difficult to spot.

Surely, many will say that he was preoccupied with the upcoming World Championship match. Although this is not impossible, I don't think it reflects the truth. In my humble opinion, it simply shows that Carlsen is only human and isn't hedged against fluctuations of form.

After the painful end of this game against Mamedyarov, I assumed that Magnus would naturally be a bit stricken for our last-round encounter, although he is known to strike back immediately after a loss. The only thing that seemed clear was that another opening surprise was surely awaiting me! I confess that I didn't expect it to happen on the second move! With 1.e4 c5 2.♘a3 he also put a smile on my face. I suppose that one of Carlsen's ideas was to drag me out of the theory as early as possible in order to lure me into time-trouble once again.

However, it didn't work out so well this time, because shortly afterwards Magnus came up with the dubious idea of leaving his king in the centre for the rest of the game. Despite spending a lot of time, I felt quite comfortable, and we soon liquidated to an endgame in which only Black could be better. I put on the pressure, and on move 34 we arrived at the following position, with me having around five minutes on the clock.

Magnus Carlsen
Nico Georgiadis
Biel 2018 (10)

position after 34.♔g4

34...♔g6?!
A very natural move that I played in less than a minute, but one that I will probably regret for quite some time. After 34...♖d3! White cannot build a good defensive set-up and is doomed to wait. Having analysed the position quite deeply, I think that White's position is lost with perfect play from both sides. However, I'll leave the final evaluation to the readers:

35.♖e2 (35.♖f1? loses to 35...♖e3, and after 35.♔h5?! ♗xg3 36.♘xg3 ♖xg3 37.♖e5 f6! 38.gxf6+ ♔xf6 39.♖xb5 e5 the e-pawn decides the game for Black) 35...♔g6

ANALYSIS DIAGRAM

Now White has two main options: 36.♖g2 ♖e3 37.♘d2 ♗c7 38.♘f3 ♖e4+ 39.♔h3 ♔h5 40.♖d2 ♖g4! 41.♖g2 a4 42.g6 ♖xg6 43.g4+ ♔h6 44.g5+ ♔h5 45.♔g4 ♖g8 46.♖h4+ ♔g6 47.♔g4 ♖d8 48.♖h6+ ♔g7 49.♖h1 ♖d5, and we've reached the same position as in the game, but without the white g3-pawn. Black now has ideas with ...♖f5 and ...♖f4+; he can bring his king to the centre and all Black's pawn are on dark squares. Black has a winning advantage. If 36.♖e1, Black must advance on the queenside with 36...b4! 37.a4, and now 37...b3! is strong. E.g. 38.♖e2 ♖d1 39.♘f2 ♖f1 40.♘h3 ♗b8, and Black will win the a-pawn with a decisive advantage.
35.♖f1!

Now the rook gets to f3 and White holds.
35...♖d3 35...b4!? was possible, but White can defend with 36.axb4 axb4 37.♖f3, and White's defensive set-up is too solid to be ruptured.
36.♖f3

36...♖d1
After 36...♖xf3 37.♔xf3 ♔f5 38.♔e3! holds!: 38...♔g4 39.♔f2 ♗c7 40.♔g2 ♗d8 41.♘d6 ♗xg5 42.♘xf7 ♗c1 43.♘d6 ♗xb2 44.♘xb5, with a draw.
37.♖f2 ♖d5?! A typical time-trouble move, after which Black has no more winning chances. 37...♖e1 would have kept some slight pressure.

38.♘d2! As soon as the knight reaches the f3-square, White can't really lose anymore.
38...♗c7 39.♘f3 ♗d8 40.♘h4 ♔g7 41.♘f3 ♗b6
With 41...♔g6 I could have repeated moves, but I saw no reason not to play on for a bit, since Black is basically running no risks.
42.♖e2 ♗c7 43.♖e4 ♗d6 44.♖d4! ♖xd4+ 45.♘xd4 b4

Here, I had expected 46.axb4, with a draw, but to my surprise, Magnus quickly played:

46.a4

Now I saw within a second that 46...bxc3 is a forced draw: 47.bxc3 ♗e5 48.♘b5 ♔g6 49.♘a3 ♗xc3 50.♘xc4, and the draw would be official.

But then, all of a sudden, I saw 46...b3, with the idea of 47...♗a3. For some reason, I couldn't find a defence for White other than 47.♘b5, which just loses. I thought for some minutes and decided to play the incredibly naive:

46...b3?? The moment I pressed the clock, I saw that White can stop the b-pawn with his knight from the d2-square and realized what I had just done. Carlsen came back from the restrooms, took a bewildered look at the position and instantly played:

47.♘f3! After which I had no other option but to resign in view of 47...♔g6 48.♘d2 ♗e7 49.♘xc4 ♗xg5 50.♘xa5 ♗c1 51.♘xb3 ♗xb2 52.a5, and the game is over.

Slap in the face

Of course, losing this game in such a way felt like a slap in the face. I have probably never felt such deep disappointment after losing a game before. I was literally unable to speak for one or two hours and very glad we didn't have to join the live commentary. It surely leaves a bitter aftertaste and I will probably regret my 46th move for a long time. Nevertheless, I would like to write down some final thoughts.

Regarding my score, I could easily have scored 2½ points instead of 1½. However, there are reasons why my

Not yet able to speak, Nico Georgiadis sportingly joins the applause when Magnus Carlsen is called to the stage at the prize-giving.

rating is just 2526 and theirs is 2750+. One needs to seize one's chances, and in chess it is unfortunately never easy to do so. When Svidler had the chance against me, he found all the best moves when it mattered to bag the full point, while I failed to do the same against Navara.

Regarding my play, I can be quite satisfied. I could have stuck to a 'hide-and-seek' strategy, which possibly would have granted me more points, but from a learning point of view that

that my opening preparation is on a pretty good level for an average GM, but compared with these guys it's just preposterous. As a result, you're most likely going to lose two or three games because you get a bad position out of the opening and they won't let you off the hook. That's what happened in my games against Mamedyarov and Vachier-Lagrave.

Summing up, despite losing the last game in such a brutal way, I'm looking back at the tournament with

'I was literally unable to speak for one or two hours and very glad we didn't have to join the live commentary.'

approach is just inferior. I tried to play aggressively and challenge the top players in an open fight. There, they mostly demonstrated their supremacy, but it was still the kind of battle in which I can learn the most.

On a more general note, I'd like to mention the high level of opening knowledge these players have. I figure

mainly positive feelings. I'm looking forward to analysing every single game deeply, and I'll try to draw the right conclusions. One conclusion I can already draw is that Biel 2018 was a truly unique opportunity for an average GM like me to cross swords with the world's best. In short, a once-in-a-lifetime experience. ■

The Ticket that was never used

FRED LUCAS

In his latest book, *Evil-Doer*, **GENNA SOSONKO** chronicles 'Half a Century with Viktor Kortchnoi', a wealth of memories and insights into the life of the great man whose trainer, colleague, friend and confidant he was. The book ends with Kortchnoi's funeral in 2016, but their special connection didn't end there, as Sosonko realized when at the end of last year a most remarkable item was put up for auction at Bubb Kuyper's in Haarlem, the Netherlands.

Some ten years ago I visited the Kaganovitch collection in Paris's Musée d'Orsay, a rather inconspicuous room (number 50) in a corner of the building containing twenty, mainly Impressionist paintings. A modest plaque told me that the room was named after Max and Rosa Kaganovitch, wealthy Parisians. In 1973, six years before he died at the age of 86, Max, a sculptor and art dealer, had left their collection to the French state and acquired immortality in that down-to-earth way.

Perhaps it was the memory of that room and a brief personal craving for immortality that inspired me when I found out in May 2011 that a Nabokov lot was to go on sale at Christie's in London. Before I knew it, the decision had made itself: London! Since one of the items in that lot was a chess set that had belonged to the famous writer.

Next to the chess pieces, protected behind glass in a museum showcase, I could already see a sign with the modest inscription 'Gift from Grandmaster Sosonko'. If neither my games

nor my books manage to secure immortality, I will try to get it on the bend with an evasive manoeuvre on the oval track (experienced cyclists will understand me, as Nabokov himself wrote in his brilliant memoir *Speak, Memory*). That sign would certainly outlive the donor.

If I could get Nabokov's chess set, I fantasized, I would give it to the Max Euwe Centre in Amsterdam. Since my entire chess archive was already gifted to this centre a long time ago, Nabokov's chess set would be one of its most impressive arte-

With an amused smile Viktor Kortchnoi listens to Genna Sosonko in the VIP room of the Amber Blindfold and Rapid tournament in Monaco in 2011.

Committee on Affairs of Censorship was located in the Nabokov house which later became the museum, and its odour still hadn't completely blown away from the premises of the museum, or from the whole country.

Having a pleasant choice for the donation, I then thought, is there a difference between the two cities in the end, since Peter the Great, who came to Holland under the name of member of the Preobrazhensky regiment Peter Mikhailov, built the city on the Neva on the Amsterdam model?

How much?

Schopenhauer couldn't stand people who came to see the house where Goethe lived, or to look at Kant's hat, instead of reading their works. He compared such people with visitors to museums who look at the pictures and pay attention only to their frames. In a way the philosopher was right, of course, but that's the way people are: you're probably also more interested in how much I paid for Nabokov's chess set than in a discussion about the place where it could have been stored. And most likely you are quite negative in general about the author's vain idea reflected in these lines, and I can understand you. I will justify myself: one of the greats claimed that even vanity can be useful – by striving for glory (even if vainly) a person subconsciously does good.

I probably haven't convinced you, and you'll be more interested in the amount I estimated the famous writer's chess set was worth. Please: £800-£1,200. That was the suggested range of the estimate for Nabokov's chess set. I found those figures on the website of Christie's, the renowned auction house that I'd walked past many times when I was in London, without ever glancing inside.

I've always liked South Kensington – I lived in that area for a month during the first half of the 1986 Kasparov-Karpov match – and

facts. And after all, the Professor was a good person, and chess in Holland owes him a lot, if not everything.

Then doubt started to overcome me: what did Euwe, Amsterdam and Holland have to do with this? No, the place for Nabokov's chess set was Bolshaya Morskaya street 47

in the museum named after him in St. Petersburg. I myself once lived in that city too, or rather, not the current me, but the one who was known by the same name almost half a century ago.

True, I was slightly bothered by the fact that in the Soviet era the

'Next to the chess pieces I already saw a sign with the modest inscription "Gift from Grandmaster Sosonko".'

now too when I'm in London I prefer to stay in that specific part of the city. Old Brompton Road, where the famous auction house is located, is the main street in that district. After booking two nights in a hotel a five-minute walk from Christie's, I began to implement my plan.

It was no secret to me that auctions usually reduce the starting price so that they can report after the bidding that the price exceeded expectations by, for example, 1.5 million! I also understood that this item was unusual, that there were no guidelines here, and that the price could soar to stratospheric heights. But if worst came to worst, I thought, after the wooden chess set in the catalogue there followed two pocket sets that had also belonged to Nabokov. One was magnetic and the other was old-fashioned – with pieces cut to fit in – the estimated price of which was lower, £400-£600. Bobby Fischer used this kind of set almost to the end.

The formula of the three D's

I was a little worried, as you always worry when you're doing something for the first time in life, but I was secretly hoping for success. After all, this wasn't Al Capone's revolver, which was sold the same year for $110,000. Or Margaret Thatcher's black handbag, which cost its new owner £25,000. And certainly it would fetch far less than the famous fluttering dress of Marilyn Monroe that was sold for $4.6 million. It's just a chess set, I thought. And a writer's chess set at that.

The chess set was only one of the items in the big Nabokov lot, which included drawings of butterflies, some of which were in books that Nabokov had given to his wife Vera. Books with Nabokov's autograph are very rare, as the writer never signed books for strangers, but only for relatives and his closest friends. In addition the lot contained butterfly nets, a desk, two typewriters with Latin and

Cyrillic letters, and other miscellaneous things that had been put up for auction by Dmitri Vladimirovich Nabokov (1934-2012), the writer's son.

As is well known, all auction houses base themselves on the formula of the three D's: death, divorce and debt. Dmitri Nabokov never married, and as for the third D, it was known that the writer's only heir constantly needed money and from time to time put his father's items and manuscripts up for auction.

A poem called 'The Ticket'

For the family of Vladimir Nabokov (1899-1977) there was no choice but exile after the Russian revolution and the defeat of the White army. In 1923, after the publication of his first foreign poetry collections, he was described as 'hostile to Soviet power' and for 60 years not one line

The Nabokov atmosphere

In his last years, Nabokov lived in the Montreux Palace Hotel, not so much out of a feeling of perpetual unsettledness that had consumed him after he left Russia, as all researchers emphasized, but out of habit. Habit? Yes, habit. Habit is a characteristic of everyone, especially people around the age of 70.

Forty years ago, in August 1976, when there was a rest day at the Interzonal tournament in Biel, Switzerland, I decided to go to Montreux, hoping to see him or even talk to him. The Nabokovs occupied several rooms on the sixth floor of the Montreux Palace Hotel. Even today you can rent the Vladimir Nabokov Suite (room 64!), consisting of a spacious room with three windows and a balcony with a view of the Alps. The hotel room (1,200 euros a night)

'After booking two nights in a hotel a five-minute walk from Christie's, I began to implement my plan.'

by Nabokov, who went under the pen-name Sirin until the Second World War, was printed in the Soviet Union. The only case requires a special explanation.

This was his poem 'The Ticket' (1927) which talked about a possible return of the poet's works to his homeland sometime. The poem attracted the attention of the proletarian troubadour Demyan Bedny, who responded in Pravda with 'A Ticket to the Other Side', a poetic feuilleton that finished with the words: 'So you're free to fantasize in Berlin, but to unclamp the Soviet jaws, you, white poet Sirin, will have to wait... till the grave is yours!' Unfortunately the prophecy of Pravda's scribbler came true – the 'Soviet jaws' didn't unclamp even after the death of the writer who had won worldwide fame.

has to be booked in advance. All the conditions of the room have been preserved and fans of living in the Nabokov atmosphere for a day can still be found.

I knew that Vladimir Vladimirovich bought Britain's *The Times* every day when he went downstairs to a nearby newspaper kiosk. It was an unusually dry, hot August, and I strolled a little around the hotel, even stopping inside, but I didn't find any Nabokov. After drinking a coffee I was about to go back to Biel, when, approaching a kiosk, I saw on the front pages of the papers the headline: *Yet another one who chose freedom!*

The various headlines repeated each other, but the point of all the reports was the same: yesterday in Amsterdam after the end of the IBM tournament a Soviet grandmaster had requested political asylum in the Netherlands. I won't say that this was so unexpected for me: hadn't Viktor Kortchnoi and I discussed this possibility in chilly Hastings in January that same year? Still, such a decisive turn of the wheel is always a surprise, especially because the day before, when we talked on the phone, Viktor hadn't made the slightest mention of his forthcoming desperate break for freedom.

When I went back to Biel, none of the participants in the tournament knew yet, but the bomb could explode at any moment. The consequences of that explosion changed the fate of many people, and determined the course of chess history for years afterwards.

A cheering smile from Nabokov

Although I had an idea of the procedures at auctions, I had never taken part in one and decided to get in touch with the management of Christie's in advance. That was the right decision. I told them straight away that I wasn't planning to buy on the phone, and that I planned to be in London myself on June 13. In that case, a woman's voice kindly advised me, I should bring only some ID and a credit card, noting that if the price of the item exceeded £30,000, a bank guarantee would be necessary. I decided not to bring a guarantee with me to London. And it wasn't because a guarantee would have burned my pocket and I could have got too involved; it's just that everything, even immortality, has its price.

Arriving an hour before the start of the bidding, I saw assistants scurrying inside the premises on Old Brompton Road, and soon the first customers started moving in too. I looked around, expecting to see perhaps Berezovsky, already living in London for many years by that time, although

I realized that people of that calibre don't go to auctions themselves, preferring to follow the bidding with the help of agents staying in phone contact with the boss. After registering I received a little sign with the number 777. I considered this a good omen, a cheering smile from Nabokov himself, if you like.

Since the crowd had arrived, I wondered when roughly the turn of the Nabokov lot would be. 'What,' a sweet young woman behind a stand said with surprise, 'don't you know that the entire Nabokov lot was sold wholesale a few days ago? But a few little things are left, shall I call the secretariat?'

From a conversation with a very nice middle-aged man in an elegant suit with a bowtie (!) only expressions like 'We very much apologize for any inconvenience, but...' remain in my memory. 'Didn't you get our email? We sent it to everyone

Their first photo together. Viktor Kortchnoi (39 at the time) and his trainer Genna Sosonko (27) at the 1970 Championship of the Soviet Union in Riga. Kortchnoi won (16/21!) ahead of Tukmakov and Stein.

who was interested in the Nabokov items.' It became obvious that although I hadn't received any email, trivial questions such as who would compensate me for my trip, pay for my hotel, my wasted time, and the main thing – my disappointment about what had happened, would be completely inappropriate.

Continuing to apologize, the assistant added that one book by the writer with his autograph remained, 'Mary', which for some reason hadn't been sold with the lot, and if I wanted it, in about an hour, when it was time for the lot... After asking as I left who on earth had bought the whole lot, and receiving in reply only a charming smile, I didn't ask any more questions. Sitting over a cappuccino in a familiar cafe nearby and looking at the no longer needed number 777, I pulled myself together and started thinking that I had incorrectly interpreted Nabokov's smile; and when I returned home I read that the assistant had been telling the truth: 'a collection of books and personal items of the writer Vladimir Nabokov was sold privately before the

start of bidding by Christie's auction house.' According to the department's expert, the price of £500,000 exceeded the overall estimate for all the lots. No, cheap immortality hasn't happened, I decided. Would such a chance come again? I had to wait six years.

A sheet of thin paper

'Among the other rubbish there is one little thing that might interest you,' I read on November 17, 2017 in an email from my colleague and Amsterdam neighbour Hans Ree. He was talking about an auction at Bubb Kuyper's in Haarlem that was starting in a couple of days, where among the varied lots with rare folios, prints, manuscripts and letters of famous writers and artists there was one with chess.

My recollections of the London failure were still fresh in my mind, but Haarlem isn't London, it's much simpler to get there from Amsterdam, and any fiasco I could encounter this time would be easier to deal with.

And... the little thing Hans Ree had mentioned had a direct relationship

to me. Its owner, who had remained in his chess post until the end, left us just two years ago, but who knew how much the things that belonged to him might be worth? He had also thought about that, and although he frowned when fans or journalists openly buttered him up in conversation, he wasn't without vanity, and he calmed Vasily Ivanchuk, who was surprised by the pencil marks in his chess books: 'Some day these books will be worth quite a lot.'

Books? No, I wasn't interested in books with his notes, especially since I have quite a few books with his autographs, some even very warm, if the word 'warm' can be used about a person who didn't lack for amorphous definitions. I also kept his letters and postcards, not to mention dozens of photographs of us together which were taken over the course of almost half a century of knowing each other. Including the very first black-and-white one, when we, very young, were standing next to each other looking at a demonstration board, discussing some position. Enlarged and given to him for his 80th birthday, the photograph hung in a frame in an honoured place in his last flat.

The lot

According to the bulky auction catalogue, in the only chess lot (it was put up for sale as a whole) there were: five medals with images of Max Euwe for his different anniversaries, two records of the 'Euwe March' from the glorious year 1935, when street organ-grinders in Amsterdam constantly repeated the uninspired tune that was written in honour of the modest girls' school mathematics teacher who overcame chess colossus Alekhine, letters from the only Dutch World Champion, a signed picture of Anatoly Karpov, a few envelopes on a chess theme with a first-day cancellation, chess stamps, including a special set issued for Euwe's 75th birthday, also with his autograph, a medal from the blind and vision-impaired World Championship that took place in Holland in 1980, a book about the Polgar family with the autographs of the three sisters and another one, by Kotov – with the Russian title 'Jokingly and seriously', and the words 'From Russia with love', written by an unknown person at an unknown time.

None of these things interested me at all (sorry Susan, Sofia, Judit, Anatoly Yevgenievch, Max Euwe, Alexander Alexandrovich Kotov, the blind and vision-impaired, philatelists and numismatists). I think that some of the items in the Haarlem auction probably would have attracted the attention of genuine collectors, but out of the whole lot I was only interested in a sheet of thin paper on which written in Latin letters was the name of the person who had called me his representative, even if to this day I don't know what he meant by that word.

Tilting their chins

It was an unusually sunny afternoon for the time of year, when on November 22, 2017, I left for one of the oldest Dutch cities. I easily found the building of the Bubb Kuyper auction house, which specializes in selling antiquarian books, manuscripts and other rarities.

I won't bore you with the procedure of the bidding, but I'll only say that after registering and looking

Two years after the date of the flight that never happened, in a small town in the Philippines, the owner of this ticket virtually single-handedly resisted a superpower that the whole world had been forced to reckon with.

their eyebrows, which meant the same thing.

Nearby there were some sharp young people with iPhones speaking in all languages (including Russian) and staying in touch with the real buyers, located God knows where. To the left of the auctioneer two young women sat behind a table with laptops, in a state of total concentration focused on their screens, and also in constant contact with clients via the Internet.

I didn't find a single person familiar to me from the chess world, thinking that most probably real chess players wouldn't be too interested in these kinds of items. Glancing at those present in the hall, by whose appear-

'Lot 2634', the auctioneer said quickly, then briefly enumerated the main items and announced the starting price. Having watched the bidding procedure already, I made a blank face and only on the third call by the auctioneer wagged my chin and raised my eyebrows just in case. Two seconds later an Internet woman raised her finger. That meant that the challenge was accepted and a counter-offer had been received. I repeated my minuscule movement – the auctioneer was already looking at me – and he immediately turned to the table, where the invisible buyer again raised the price. This action repeated itself several times until the woman, without averting her eyes from the screen, didn't raise her finger for some time, and then shook her head.

'One! Two! Three!' exclaimed the auctioneer, and the hammer blow announced that the owner of the chess lot was your humble servant.

The flight that never happened

After paying and receiving a small box, I impatiently went into the nearest cafe and first of all checked for the presence of the only item that had brought me to the Haarlem auction. It was an unused ticket for an Aeroflot Amsterdam-Moscow flight.

'This action repeated itself several times until the woman, without averting her eyes from the screen, didn't raise her finger for some time, and then shook her head.'

around, I noticed that experienced buyers didn't raise a hand with their number, but just tilted their chins, showing the auctioneer, who noticed every movement, that the bid had increased. Others raised

ance I couldn't have immediately determined their type of occupation, and the alert iPhone guys and women at the Internet table, I calculated from which direction I could expect danger.

Finally it was the turn of the chess lot.

'A new page in the battle for the World Championship began, comparable in its intensity with the direct confrontation between East and West during the Spassky-Fischer match in 1972.'

Nothing special – a ticket is a ticket, and the flight for July 27, 1976 was even already confirmed, as evidenced by the letters OK on the glued-in page, as they used to do it. But it was pleasant to hold the ticket in my hands, and I looked through the wonderfully-preserved pages in the blue cover, trying to feel immersed in the history.

A gaping hole and a crater

Forty-two years ago that unused ticket not only left a gaping hole in Soviet chess, but also soon became the crater of an active volcano that forced not only the functionaries of the chess federation and Sports Committee to worry considerably, but also the brass at the very top of the pyramid of power in the Soviet Union.

Two years after the date of the flight that never happened, in a small town in the Philippines, the owner of this ticket virtually single-handedly resisted a superpower that the whole world had been forced to reckon with. The giant state mobilized against him an entire army of coaches, consultants, advisors, journalists, translators, overt and covert KGB agents, functionaries of all ranks, doctors, psychologists and masseurs. Moreover, this state still had his family as hostages, and for many it seemed like a miracle that this person was in any condition to play chess.

From the date dispassionately registered on the ticket a new page in the battle for the World Championship began, comparable in its intensity with the direct confrontation between East and West during the Spassky-Fischer match in 1972.

The fact that a former Soviet citizen was representing the West gave this merciless battle a particular sharpness.

Chess always enjoyed unbelievable popularity in the enormous empire that was isolated from the rest of the world, and this was a four-time champion of the country, a fierce and legendary warrior, the name of whom was known to everyone. Regularly facing representatives of the Soviet Union in Candidates' matches and duels for the world crown, the Evil-Doer, as he was immediately dubbed in his former homeland, constantly reminded millions of his former compatriots about his existence.

I was thinking about all that while holding the well-preserved pieces of paper in my hands. But it was strange: I didn't have a sense of euphoria that this ticket now belonged to me, and very soon I was consumed with a feeling similar to that of an experienced Lothario for whom the process of seduction itself is important, while its result can only be compared with getting stitches after a successful operation.

On the other hand, I thought, there are many copies of the Mona Lisa, and they're incredibly varied – postcards, cartoons, posters, images on T-shirts and chocolate boxes, but the painting itself can only be seen in the Louvre, even if millions of tourists from all over the world fill its rooms.

Frame, donate, or?

It's not out of place to say that I've never collected anything in my life. I don't keep medals or tokens, pennants, certificates or cups. True, my only one – for winning the zonal tournament in Barcelona in 1975 – gathered dust in the shed for a long time and was already covered in rust, but recently I gave that one too to someone who is keen on those kinds of knick-knacks.

Soon I was visited by a thought about what to do with the ticket, which had been put away somewhere on a shelf in the same auction box together with the other items that were useless to me. Someone advised me to order a frame and hang the ticket in my study next to our photograph from Riga in long-ago December 1970, and others thought I should just wait for better times, as the prices for these kinds of items only go up.

Or perhaps, after all, give the ticket to the Max Euwe Centre, which was unlucky with Nabokov's chess set? As the unused ticket was from Amsterdam, and the then-FIDE president was a direct participant in the fate of the defector.

Or donate an exhibit to the chess museum of the Central Chess Club in Moscow, where on the evening of July 27, 1976 'Korchnoi V.L. MR' was due to land and didn't land.

True, after his death, in some Russian obituaries I read about the departure of 'a top Soviet grandmaster' and was sure that this phrase would have made him extremely angry. And in the climate of today's Russia the museum on Gogol Boulevard in Moscow would probably send the ticket straight into storage. A little more, and Kortchnoi will turn into the Evil-Doer again: in a country where many of the institutions of Soviet power have been revived, saying a bad word about those glorious times is hardly celebrated.

Or perhaps go to the Amsterdam office of Aeroflot and, presenting the ticket, ask for compensation: never mind that over 40 years have passed since that time, the ticket is still unused.

Truly, I don't know. ∎

MAXIMize your Tactics

with Maxim Notkin

Find the best move in the positions below

Solutions on page 95

1. Black to move

2. Black to move

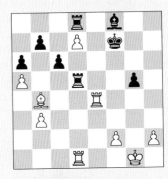

3. White to move

4. White to move

5. White to move

6. White to move

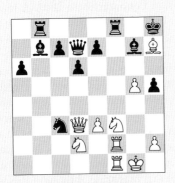

7. White to move

8. White to move

9. White to move

CANDIDATE MOVES

Summer is known in British media circles as the 'silly season', when frivolity takes the place of serious journalism. Apparently this tradition exists in Greece too, as the aspiring FIDE President, Georgios Makropoulos, chose the month of August to remind us all – but himself mainly – that he was once a chess player, by publishing an antique combination of his own on his Facebook campaign page.

The sacrificial finish to his game against Kallai, from 1984, was moderately pretty, but by no means difficult (36.♖g3 ♖xg3 37.♕xg3 ♗g7 38.♘g6+ hxg6 39.♕h4+ ♗h6 40.♕xh6 mate). The one thing that made this otherwise unexceptional posting noteworthy was the eye-catching appreciation of Hellenic aesthetics by some 3,000+ bots – an observation not lost on the ACP President, Emil Sutovsky, who called his 'fake likes campaign' a 'new low of (the) current FIDE leadership'.

Predictably, this induced a furious response from Makro. Given that the official 'program' of his campaign is entirely devoid of policy other than claiming that he is 'honest' (presumably in the same sense as Iago, from Shakespeare's play Othello) and is predicated upon stating that his coronation is a foregone conclusion, upon the basis of non-existent or bogus statistics, it is understandable that this accusation should have struck a very raw nerve. Makropoulos lashed back with the imputation that Sutovsky was 'displaying vulgar behaviour' and had 'low IQ' too.

Words are just weapons with Makro and rarely, if ever, have any inherent meaning. The utter imbecility of his argument can be gauged from the following statements:

'Emil, what you still fail to understand is that I am not seeking support from facebook.'

To just two sentences later:

'We are promoting our campaign via facebook page ads, to much larger audience of chess fans, because we think that this is the right thing to do.'

Quite.

It is rather like when I remarked on Twitter that 'hypocrite' was a Greek word, to which Makro replied that my Greek was 'inaccurate'. This somewhat contentious, if not to say deliberately misleading, linguistic argument led my (Greek) wife to ask whether the national champion had finished high school. A short while later, without the slightest apology or acknowledgement that he was flatly contradicting himself, he admitted that 'hypocrite' was indeed a Greek word, and not Sumerian or Aramaic.

'Why does he say things which can be so obviously disproven?', asked Peter Heine Nielsen, in another context. Because the sort of people who vote for Makro really don't care about shameless mendacity, is the short and simple answer.

While your columnist has nothing to compare with the peerless beauty of a Makropoulos combination, this may be a good moment to fulfill an old promise. In my column in New In Chess 2016/8, I wrote about the secret match I played against Ruslan Ponomariov in 2003. A match without spectators – barring the stuffed animals on the walls – in a hunting lodge with a leaking roof in the Crimean coastal town of Yalta.

In that column I showed my win in an Evans Gambit in Game 6 and made the following reference to the eighth and final game (when the match was already decided, as Ponomariov was leading 4½-2½): '... one of the most chaotic, thrilling, ingenious, blunderful games of my entire career. Pieces perished in an orgiastic hecatomb. (...) I would love to annotate it one day, and no doubt I will, on the pages of this magazine.' I thought this was an apt moment to do so.

Nigel Short
Ruslan Ponomariov
Yalta training match 2003 (8)
Evans Gambit

**1.e4 e5 2.♘f3 ♘c6 3.♗c4 ♗c5
4.b4!?** Again I chose to play the Evans Gambit, a very risky decision despite my success in Game 6. In general it is wiser to keep such speculative openings as surprise weapons. However, the fact that we were not playing for either money or rating

8.dxe5 The most direct, although there exist other non-too convincing tries.
8...♗b6 9.♘bd2 9.a4 was the preference of Hikaru Nakamura against Vishy Anand at the 2014 London Chess Classic. It led to a fairly insipid draw.
9...♘a5 Perfectly adequate, but there is a strong argument for the cold-blooded and materialistic 9...dxe5 as recommended by Larry Christiansen

13...♕g4!?
Ambitious! The direct 13...g5! 14.♘xb6 axb6 15.♗g3 dxe4 16.♕xe4 ♘e7 was absolutely fine. White has all sorts of positional weaknesses, but perhaps the insecurity of the black king is a slight concern.
14.0-0-0
Still optimistically hoping for a Morphy finish.
14...g5 15.e6!
With two pieces en prise White sacrifices a pawn to free the e5-square for a knight! It is actually the only playable move in the position, but now it gets seriously complicated.
The uninspired retreat 15.♘xb6 axb6 16.♗g3 ♕xe4 was obviously no good.

> **'One of the most chaotic, thrilling, ingenious, blunderful games of my entire career. Pieces perished in an orgiastic hecatomb.'**

made me a tad more reckless than usual. Besides, I was genuinely curious to see what he had prepared.
**4...♗xb4 5.c3 ♗a5 6.d4 d6
7.♕b3**

in *Inside Chess* many moons ago. His much younger countryman, Fabiano Caruana, also favours such greed.
10.♕c2 ♘xc4 11.♘xc4 d5

7...♕d7 The Conservative Defence, as the name implies, is undoubtedly one of Black's most solid options. Interestingly, the apparent blunder 7...♕e7 is also playable, although somewhat loose, after 8.d5 ♘d4! (8...♘b8? 9.♕a4++—has occurred in more than one simul game of mine – the last time in Gaborone 2017).

12.♗g5!? An attempt to inject a bit of life into the position. The alternative 12.exd5 ♕xd5 13.♕a4+ ♗d7 14.♘xb6 cxb6 15.♕d4 ♘e7 is not at all inspiring.
12...h6 Obviously not falling for 12...dxc4? 13.♖d1, with a Morphy-Duke of Brunswick mate on d8 in the offing.
13.♗h4

15...♗xe6
There were an awful lot of things to consider.
15...♕f4+ 16.♖d2 gxh4 wins a piece, but then:

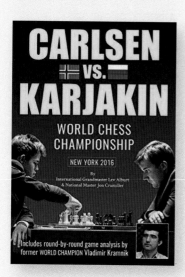

ANALYSIS DIAGRAM

17.exd5! fxe6 (17...♕xc4? leads to a lost position after 18.♘e5 ♕f4 19.exf7+ ♕xf7 (19...♔d8 20.♕e4!!) 20.♘xf7 ♔xf7 21.d6 ♘f6 22.♖e1 and Black cannot defend, e.g. 22...cxd6 23.♖xd6 ♗c5 24.♕b3+ ♔g6 25.♖xf6+ ♔xf6 26.♕d5 ♗a3+ 27.♔c2 ♗f5+ 28.♔b3 ♗f8 29.♕e5+) 18.dxe6 ♕f6 19.♕a4+ ♔f8 20.♘xb6 cxb6 21.♖e1 ♗xe6 22.♖e3 and White has more than sufficient compensation for the piece deficit.

17.♕a4+ ♔f8 18.exd5, threatening 19.♘xb6, was my original idea, and it is also pretty dangerous, e.g. 18...♗c5 19.♘fe5 (intending 20.♘d3! among other things). My engine claims this is completely equal, but good luck to you if you ever have to defend this in a game. Surprisingly 15...fxe6! might be the best move, e.g. 16.♕a4+ ♗d7 17.♕xd7+ ♔xd7 18.♘ce5+ ♔d6! 19.♘xg4 gxh4 20.exd5 exd5 21.♘xh4 c6 with equality.

16.exd5

16...♗d7 Or 16...♕xc4 17.dxe6 gxh4 18.♖he1! (stronger than the straight-forward 18.exf7+ ♕xf7 19.♖he1+ ♘e7 20.♕a4+ c6 21.♕b4, with a murky position) 18...f5 (18...fxe6 19.♕g6+ ♔f8 20.♖d3! ♕f4+ 21.♘d2! and White is winning; 18...♘e7? 19.♖e4! ♕b5

20.exf7+ with a decisive onslaught, e.g. 20...♔f8 21.♖xe7 ♔xe7 22.♕e4+ ♔f8 23.♘e5) 19.♘e5 ♕f4+ 20.♔b1 ♘e7 21.♖d7, with superb attacking prospects.

17.♖he1+ The simple 17.♘xb6 axb6 18.♗g3, as suggested by Ruslan after the game, leaves Black in huge trouble, but the text is stronger still.

17...♔f8

18.♖e4?? An horrific blunder. Here is where my tactical skills failed completely.

Correct was 18.♘ce5! ♕f4+ 19.♖d2 ♗a4 20.♕d3 gxh4 21.♖e4! ♕f5 22.♘xh4 ♕g5 23.♘hg6+! (23.♘ef3 ♕f6 24.♖xa4 wins simply and far more humanly) 23...fxg6 24.h4 ♕xe5 (24...♕f6 25.♖f4) 25.♖xe5 ♖e8 26.♕f3+ ♔g7 27.♕e4, with an overwhelming position.

18...♕f5? Instead, 18...♕xg2! 19.♘e1 ♕xh2! (19...♕h3 20.♖d3) 20.♗g3 ♕h3 grabs material and discombobulates the White forces.

19.g4! 19.♗g3 ♘f6 20.♘xb6 axb6 21.♖ed4 ♕xc2+ 22.♔xc2 ♗a4+ 23.♖xa4 ♖xa4 24.♗e5 is apparently playable, although I did not see this at all.

19...♕h7 19...♕xf3 runs into 20.♘e5.
20.♘fe5 ♗e8 21.♕e2! ♘f6
21...gxh4 22.d6 cxd6 23.♘xd6 leads to an attack of extraordinary ferocity.

22.♖f4!! The star move of the game. It is not often that a player gets to fork his own pieces!
22...♕g7 The only move. 22...gxf4 23.♗xf6 is just hopeless.
23.d6 ♔g8 23...gxf4 24.d7 ♘xd7 25.♖xd7 leads to much the same thing: 25...♗xd7? (25...♔g8) 26.♘xd7+ ♔g8 27.♘f6+ ♔f8 28.♘e5, winning.
24.d7 ♘xd7 25.♖xd7 gxf4

26.♕f3?? Here I became regrettably carried away with my own genius. When you are sacrificing one piece after another it is sometimes difficult just to stop and play normal moves. I made a similar psychological error in Game 8 of my World Championship match with Kasparov, when a simple quiet continuation would have won after a cascade of sacrifices. The obvious 26.♖e7 leaves White with a huge advantage. Black is totally discoordinated and can do little to impede the increasing pressure.
26...♗xd7 Seizing his chance.
27.♘xd7 ♗e3+! 28.♔b2

28...♗d4!! Cunningly defending f6!
29.♔b3! ♗xc3! 30.♕xc3 ♕xc3+ 31.♔xc3

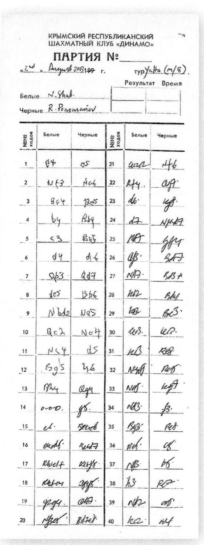

Nigel Short's score sheet. Having woken up with a painful trapped nerve in his right elbow, he had to write down the moves of Game 8 with his left hand.

Now a new endgame phase begins. Black still has some trouble coordinating, despite the vastly reduced material. Objectively he stands well though.
31...♖e8 32.♘ce5

32...♖xe5?! Apparently I was not the only one obsessed with sacrificing material unnecessarily. Correct is 32...h5!, after which it is hard to keep a lid on Black's play. He can try with 33.♗f6! hxg4 34.♗xh8 ♔xh8 35.♘xf7+ ♔g7 36.♘fe5 ♗e7 37.♘d4 and the knights form a strong defensive barrier.
33.♘xe5 ♔g7 34.♘d3 f3?! Again Black should strike with 34...h5!.
35.♗g3 ♖e8 36.♘e5 c5 37.♘xf3 b5

Here Ruslan thought he stood better, whereas I thought I had the edge. God, however, says that it is equal.

38.h3 ♖e2 39.♘d2 a5 40.♔c2 a4 41.♔d1 ♖e6 42.♗f4! A nice move, aiming to place the bishop on its optimum square e3. **42...♔g6?!** Natural, but a first small step in the wrong direction. **43.♗e3 ♖e5 44.♔c2 h5 45.♘f3 ♖d5 46.♘e1! hxg4 47.hxg4 c4 48.♔c3**

It is now starting to get difficult for Black. **48...f5** Apparently 48...♖d1 49.♘c2 ♖b1 was necessary. **49.♘g2** Better was 49.g5!. **49...♖d3+ 50.♔b4**

50...fxg4? I thought this move drew at the time, but I can now say with certainty that it loses.

50...♔f7! was the way to keep Black in the game.

51.♘f4+ ♔f5 52.♘xd3 cxd3 53.♔c3 ♔e4 54.♗c5

54...♔d5

This loses without a prayer, but it would have been far more critical to test my skills with 54...♔f3 55.♔xd3 g3 56.fxg3 ♔xg3.

ANALYSIS DIAGRAM

I had erroneously assumed that this was the Kortchnoi-Karpov endgame from Baguio City and therefore drawn, but the fact that White's pawn is on a2 and not a3 makes all the difference. It was interesting that when I first showed this game to Garry Kasparov, in St. Louis, some years ago, he scratched his head for a few minutes and came to the correct assessment. The winning method is, in my opinion, far from trivial. Would I have found it? I have no idea.

The following is, of course, with the help of tablebases: 57.♔c3 ♔f4 58.♔b4 ♔e5 59.♔xb5 ♔d5 60.♗b4 ♔e6 61.♔c6 ♔e5 62.♔d7 ♔f6 63.♗d6 ♔f5 64.♔e7 ♔g6 65.♔e6 ♔g5 66.♗e5 ♔g6 67.♗f6 ♔h6 68.♔f7 ♔h5 69.♗e7 ♔g4 70.♔e6 ♔f4 71.♗f6 ♔g4 72.♔e5 ♔h5 73.♔f5 ♔h6 74.♗d4 ♔h7 75.♔f6 ♔h6 76.♗e3+ ♔h5 77.♔f5 ♔h4 78.♗f4 ♔h3 79.♗g5 ♔g3 80.a3!

ANALYSIS DIAGRAM

Only now does this work! 80...♔f3 81.♗f4 ♔g2 82.♔g4 ♔f2 83.♗c1 ♔e2 84.♔f4 ♔d3 85.♔e5 ♔c4

ANALYSIS DIAGRAM

86.♗e3!! (the only winning move – 86.♔d6? ♔d4! 87.♔c6 ♔e5! and the king races back to a8) 86...♔b3 87.♔c5 ♔c4 88.♔d6 ♔b5 89.♗e3 ♔a6 90.♔c6 ♔a5 91.♔b7 ♔b5 92.♗b6 ♔c4 93.♔c6 ♔b3 94.♗c5 ♔c4 95.♗d6 ♔d4 96.♔b5 ♔d5 97.♗h2 ♔e6 98.♔xa4 ♔d7 99.♔b5 ♔c8 100.♔b6 and White wins.

55.♗e7 ♔e4 56.♔d2 ♔f3 57.♗h4 ♔e4 58.a3 ♔d4 59.♗g5 ♔c4 60.♗f6 ♔b3 61.♗e7 ♔c4 62.♗e3 ♔c3 63.♗f8

Zugzwang beckons.

63...b4 A last try. Both 63...♔c4 and 63...♔c2 are met by 64.♗b4.

64.♗xb4+ ♔c2 65.♗d2 ♔b3 66.♔xd3 ♔xa3 67.♔c2

Black resigned.

It was very weird how my bishop that was en prise for 11 consecutive moves should somehow survive and win the day.

Nigel Short

NEW FROM GAMBIT

Just released: **Chess Studio 2**, a thoroughly redesigned, rewritten and updated version of Gambit's enhanced chess e-book reader, available for Android and Apple mobile devices.

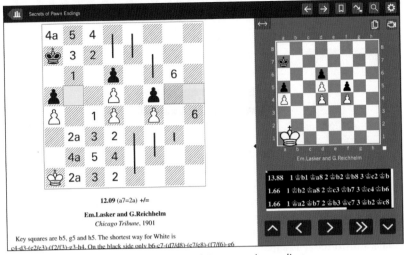

The engine helps explain a complex ending

- Powerful analysis engine
- Display options include a resizable live board and colour schemes
- More flexible ways to play over the chess moves on the live board
- Portrait and landscape mode
- Enter moves on the live board
- Create your own named bookmarks
- Tested with a wide range of tablets, phones and emulators
- New free sampler
- Improved bookstore functions
- Search for "gambit chess studio" on Google Play or the Apple App Store

All new books from Gambit are available immediately on the Chess Studio app, together with more than 100 backlist titles, and over 20 in German language. You don't need a set or board – see all the positions and play all the moves just by tapping on the screen. The app is free – try before you buy! The books available are suitable for all ages and cover all aspects of chess – openings, tactics, strategy, endgames and more. They range from our bestselling kids books to specialist titles for experts and masters. Prices range from $4.99 to $14.99, and once you've bought a book, you can read it on all your compatible devices. A whole chess library in the palm of your hand!

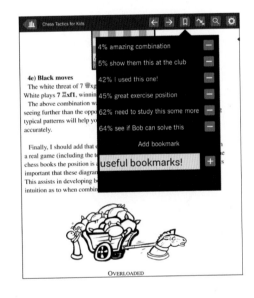

"I just updated to Chess Studio 2 on a Chromebook, and am really liking the keyboard navigation, and computer analysis features! Looks great so far ... Looking forward to more good books." – Tom Unger

"Excellent upgrade ... [We've] been waiting for this upgrade for a long time. Great!" – Lúcio Casado Silva

Latest titles in print and on Chess Studio:

Applying Logic in Chess
Erik Kislik

A top trainer demystifies modern chess thinking in this thought-provoking, thoroughly modern and original work. New insights include true piece values, improvement methods and opening preparation in the modern era.

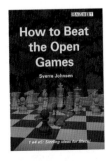

How to Beat the Open Games
Sverre Johnsen

Famed opening writer Johnsen explains a full repertoire for Black with 1 e4 e5 when White avoids the Ruy Lopez. Cutting-edge developments in the Giuoco Piano and Scotch, together with a firm grounding in the traditional lines.

gambitbooks.com

Shirov's Shocker in the Rubinstein French

Jeroen Bosch

5.g4!?

'Gains space, anticipates a knight arriving on f6 and enables the king's bishop to move to the long diagonal. Not bad for one move!'

One of the most solid ways to combat 1.e4 is the Rubinstein Variation of the French. True, Black's third move is a major concession: he surrenders the centre. In return, however, he gets a well-defined pawn structure, simple development and a clear equalizing plan. White really has to make an effort to meet the sequence ...♘d7, ...♘gf6, ...♗e7, ...0-0, ...c5 convincingly. Enter Alexei Shirov for a real shocker on move 5!
1.e4 e6 2.d4 d5 3.♘c3 dxe4 4.♘xe4 ♘d7 5.g4!?

Modern chess has seen so many early g4-thrusts that this is perhaps less of a shock than I advertised in the title. And yet, for a classical player educated in the games of, say, Rubinstein, there seems to be neither rhyme nor reason behind White's last move.

The main line of the Rubinstein goes 5.♘f3 ♘gf6 6.♘xf6+ ♘xf6 7.♗d3 c5, with thousands upon thousands of games played, and a verdict that hovers between ± and =. If you want to fianchetto the bishop, the modest 5.g3 feels adequate, a logical continuation being 5...♘gf6 6.♘xf6+ ♘xf6 7.♗g2 c5. Note that those in the know (Wesley So, Rubinstein expert Georg Meier, Rustam Kasimdzhanov) actually meet 5.g3 with 5...♗e7!? 6.♗g2 ♘gf6 7.♘xf6+ ♗xf6! 8.♘f3 0-0 9.0-0 e5, with a symmetrical structure and almost nothing but draws.

Let's approach 5.g4 in a positive spirit: it gains space, anticipates a knight arriving on f6 (which will be chased away with g4-g5) and enables the king's bishop to move to the long diagonal. Not bad for one move! On the downside, 5.g4 may weaken White's set-up a bit and slows down his development.

Let's remind ourselves of how Alekhine once played against Euwe (7th match game of the 1935 World Championship): 1.e4 e6 2.d4 d5 3.♘c3 ♗b4 4.♘ge2 dxe4 5.a3 ♗e7 6.♘xe4 (Swedish GM Jonny Hector likes 6.g4!) 6...♘c6 7.g4!?.

Taking all this into account, and combined with the solid reputation of the Rubinstein, I would like to echo Anish Giri, who, on the 7th of May of this year (when Shirov played 5.g4 versus Alekseev), tweeted the position with a 'Why not?' followed by a cool emoticon.

5...♘gf6

Business as usual. Black just continues his regular development scheme, aiming to trade a pair of knights to make good on his space disadvantage.

There are other, more subtle replies that we should also take into consideration.

■ First of all, there is 5...♖b8!?, when Shirov and Sulskis have simply played 6.♗g2 b5 (or 6...b6, transposing to Makepeace-Webster, Swansea 2006, which started with 5...b6) 7.♕e2 (7.♘f3 ♗b7 8.♕e2 a6 9.0-0 ♘gf6 10.♘xf6+ ♘xf6 11.g5 ♘d7 12.a4 ♗d6 13.axb5 axb5 14.♘e5 ♗xg2 15.♔xg2 ♘xe5 16.dxe5 0-0 was equal in the blitz game Shirov-Meier, Berlin 2018) 7...♗b7 8.♗d2 ♗e7 9.0-0-0!, allowing his opponent into winning a piece!

9...f5?! 10.d5! fxe4 (Black loses after 10...exd5? 11.♘g5+–; and 10...♗xd5 11.gxf5 exf5 12.♗c3! – 12.♘d6+ cxd6 13.♗xd5± – 12...♘c4 13.♕h5+ g6 14.♕h3 is no better) 11.dxe6 ♘b6

12.♗c3 (12.♕xb5+! is probably objectively stronger) 12...♗g5+? 13.♔b1 ♕e7 (13...♗d5 14.♗xe4 ♘f6 15.♗f3, with h4 and g5 coming up, demonstrates why the intermediate check was so bad) 14.♗xe4 ♗xe4 15.♕xe4 ♘f6 16.♕c6+ ♔f8 17.♘h3, with a winning attack in Sulskis-Maric, Dubai 2005. Better than 12...♗g5+ is 12...♗d5! 13.♗xe4 (or 13.♗xg7 ♗f6 14.g5! ♗xg7 15.♕h5+ ♔e7 16.♕f7+ ♔d6 17.♕xg7, and White has an ongoing attack with sufficient compensation for the material deficit) 13...♘f6 14.♗xd5 ♘bxd5 15.♕f3 (not 15.g5? ♘xc3 16.♖xd8+ ♖xd8 17.bxc3 ♗a3+ 18.♔b1 ♘e4, and Black wins) 15...c6 16.g5 0-0, and Black returns the material with an equal position.

But let's return to 5...♖b8. Now that Black has signposted his intention to trade bishops along the long diagonal, I would prefer to stay flexible and play 6.♘f3!?

– when 6...♘gf6 7.♘xf6+ ♘xf6 8.g5 is similar to our main line, but Black has committed himself to an early ...♖b8;
– and 6...b5 can be met by 7.♗d3! ♗b7 8.g5! ♘e7 9.♕e2, with at least a very interesting position that strikes me as better for White.

■ I don't think Black can afford the immediate equalizing attempt 5...e5 6.♘f3!? (6.dxe5! looks simply somewhat better for White) 6...♘gf6 (White is also slightly better after 6...exd4 7.♕xd4 ♘gf6) 7.♕e2 ♕e7 (7...♘xe4 8.♕xe4 ♗e7 9.dxe5 ♘c5 10.♕d4± , rather than 10.♕f4 0-0!, and Black has compensation for the pawn) 8.♘xf6+ gxf6

9.g5?! (9.♖g1! is stronger) 9...e4 10.gxf6 ♘xf6 11.♘e5 ♖g8 was dynamically balanced in Abreu Delgado-Perez Garcia, Havana 2005.

■ After 5...b6 it makes no sense to play 6.♘f3 (compared to 5...♖b8 6.♘f3 Black has not wasted a tempo on ...♖b8 yet, so he develops quickly) 6...♗b7 7.♗d3 ♘gf6 is very fine for Black, of course. So White should consider 6.♗g2 ♖b8 7.g5!?,

taking advantage of the fact that Black has delayed ...♘gf6 (and, of course, that we have played 5.g4).

■ In case of the very subtle 5...♗e7 (please remember that this was how Meier and So replied to 5.g3), White can really take advantage of our 'extended fianchetto' with 6.g5!.

6.♘xf6+

Once you have played a move like 5. g4, it makes sense to keep up some pace.

In practice, 6.♘g3 (so as not to trade pieces) has also been played, but this is time-consuming. 6...c5 7.g5 ♘d5 (stronger than 7...♘g8 8.♘f3 ♗e7 9.♗g2 ♕c7 10.0-0 ♘g6. Black won in J.Snuverink-Harff, Maastricht 2014. However, if White had continued with 11.♖e1 ♗e7 12.h4 – 12.d5 0-0! – 12...0-0 – 12...♘f4? 13.♗xf4 ♕xf4 14.d5 – 13.♘e2, he would have been better) 8.♗g2 cxd4 9.♕xd4

9...♘b4 (the chances are about equal after 9...♕b6) 10.♕c3 ♕a5 11.♗d2 ♕e5+ 12.♕xe5 ♘xe5 13.0-0-0 ♗d7 was a tad better for White in Sulskis-Pelletier, Porto Carras 2011. Note that White has enough compensation for the pawn (his edge in development!) after 13...♘xa2+ 14.♔b1.

After 6.♘g3, I would be tempted as Black to play the simple 6...h6, followed by ...c5.

6...♘xf6 7.g5

Again, this is the most consistent continuation of the plan started on move 5.

Practice has also seen 7.♗g2

and now:

■ 7...h6 8.h4 c5 9.g5 hxg5 10.hxg5 ♖xh1 11.♗xh1 ♘d5 12.♘f3 ♗e7?! (12...cxd4 13.♕xd4 ♘b4) 13.c4± 13...♘b6 14.b3 ♗d7?! 15.♘e5 cxd4?!, and here 16.♕xd4 was good enough in H.Urban-S.Müller, DDR 1976, but 16.♕h5! would have been even stronger.

■ 7...e5 8.g5 ♘d7 9.dxe5 ♘xe5 10.♕xd8+ ♔xd8 11.♗f4 (11.♘e2) 11...♗d6 (11...♗b4+!, when White has to forego castling, since 12.c3? fails to 12...♘d3+) 12.0-0-0 ♖e8 13.♘f3, and Black was in huge trouble in a Grischuk simul, Grischuk-Krain, Mainz 2005.

■ Black has 7...c5 and 7...♗e7 as very decent replies to 7.♗g2.

7...♘d5

This is the normal reply.

■ The intermediate 7...♕d5 is playable, although White is slightly better in the queenless middlegame after 8.♘f3 ♕e4+ 9.♕e2 ♕xe2+ 10.♗xe2 (10.♔xe2!?, to place the bishop on the long diagonal, also promises a slight edge)

10...♘d7 11.♗e3 ♗d6 12.♘d2 b6 13.♘c4 (13.♘f3!? ♖b8 14.0-0-0 ♗b7 15.♗xb7 ♖xb7 16.c4±) 13...♗b7

14.♘xd6+ cxd6 15.♖g1 ♔e7 16.♔d2 ♖ac8 17.a4. White has the bishop pair and more space, although Black is still solid, of course, Izoria-Yang, Philadelphia 2013.

■ 7...♘e4 8.♗d3 (more accurate looks 8.♘f3 ♘d6 9.♗d3) 8...♘d6 (Black could have exploited White's move order with 8...♕d5!?, intending 9.♘f3 ♗b4+!) 9.♘f3 b6 10.♖g1 ♗b7

11.♘e5 (alternatives are 11.♕e2 or 11.c3) 11...g6?! (understandable, but now White gets a pleasant game; stronger was 11...♗f5, as 12.♗b5+ – 12.c3 ♗d6 – 12...c6! 13.♘xc6 fails tactically to 13...♕d5!) 12.c3 ♗g7 13.♗f4 a6 14.♕e2 ♕e7 15.♘g4 ♔d7?! (this looks very odd, but Black has problems with his king anyway – 15...0-0 16.h4; 15...0-0-0 16.♗xa6), 16.0-0-0, with a superior game, Kislinsky-Ivaschenko, Alushta 2011.

■ Nobody has tried 7...♘d7 yet, although it makes sense, since it prepares ...c5.

8.♗g2

Kislinsky has played 8.a3 to prepare c4, but this should hardly promise an edge after moves like 8...♗d7 9.c4 ♘e7, 8...♗e7, or 8...c5. Instead, Kislinsky-Stupak, Gora Swietej Anny 2016, went 8...h6 9.g6!? fxg6 10.♗d3 ♕f6 11.c4 ♘e7 12.♘f3 ♘f5 (12...♗d7) 13.♖g1 ♗d7 14.♘e5 0-0-0 15.♖xg6 ♕e7 16.♕g4, with chances for both sides.

Naturally, White can also play 8.♘f3 when, after 8...c5, 9.♗g2 transposes to our main line. The game Shirov-Alekseev, Sochi 2018, instead went 9.c4 ♘e7 10.dxc5 ♕xd1+ 11.♔xd1 ♘f5 12.c6! bxc6 13.♗d3. The chances are equal here, but there are enough unbalancing factors to guarantee a fully-fledged fight.

For example:
– 13...♗b7 14.♗xf5 0-0-0+ (14...exf5 15.♖e1+ ♔e7 16.♗f4 c5 17.♘d2) 15.♔c2 exf5 (15...c5 16.♖e1 ♗xf3?! 17.♗e4±) 16.♘e5 c5 17.♖e1 ♖e8 18.♗f4, and despite Black's bishop pair, White is not worse, e.g. 18...♗e4+ 19.♔c3 ♗d6 20.♘g6.
– 13...g6 14.♗f4 h6 15.♗e5 ♖h7 16.♔c2?! was Shirov-Alekseev. After this move Black even got a slight edge with 16...♗b7; the centralizing 16.♔e2 would have kept things balanced.

8...c5 Black's typical Rubinstein counter in the centre.
However, since White has placed his bishop on the long diagonal, it also makes sense to try and cement the knight on d5 with 8...b5!?.
9.♘f3
Slightly more passive is 9.♘e2, which doesn't obstruct the bishop's diagonal. After 9...♗e7 10.dxc5 ♕a5+ 11.c3 ♕xc5 12.♕d4 0-0 13.♕xc5 ♗xc5, 14.♘f4 is a tiny bit better for White. Instead, the game Mirosh-

nichenko-Popovich, Alushta 1999, went 14.♘g3?! ♗d7 15.♗xd5?! exd5 16.♗e3∓.
Although we have played only plausible moves after 5.g4, this position has only been reached once – ample proof that there is plenty of room for creativity after our SOS reply against the Rubinstein!

9...♕c7 10.0-0 ♘f4
Ambitious and positionally sound, but White now gets a strong lead in development, so it would have been safer to settle for 10...♗e7.
11.♗xf4 ♕xf4 12.♕d3!

Connecting the rooks and threatening 13.♕b5+.
12...♗d7 13.♖fe1
Not bad either is 13.♖ad1!?, intending to meet 13...♗c6 with 14.♘e5! ♗xg2 (White is still better in the double rook ending after 14...♗d6 15.♕e3 ♗xe5 16.♕xe5 ♕xe5 17.♗xc6+ bxc6 18.dxe5) 15.♔xg2, and now 15...♕xg5+? is bad in view of 16.♔h1, and Black is in trouble.
13...♗d6?!
13...♗c6 14.d5! is also far better for White. 13...♗e7 14.♘e5 is annoying for Black, but 13...♖d8! is the most

accurate move, when Black may still preserve the balance.
14.♖e4 Equally strong is 14.dxc5 ♗xc5 15.♕c3.
14...♕f5?! Best was 14...c4! 15.♕e2 ♕f5, when White keeps the initiative with 16.♘e5!.
15.♖ae1! 0-0? Black probably had to settle for losing a pawn with 15...0-0-0 16.dxc5 ♗c7 (not 16...♗xc5? 17.♖c4, and White wins a piece). Please note that the intermediate 15...c4 is met by 16.♖xe6+! (16.♕xc4 ♗c6) 16...♕xe6 17.♕xc4.

16.dxc5! Winning material! **16...♗c6** 16...♗xc5 17.♕xd7; 16...♕xc5 17.♖d4.
17.cxd6 ♗xe4 18.♖xe4 ♖fd8
The rest is a massacre:
19.♘e5 ♕xg5 20.f4 ♕h5 21.♖e3 ♖ab8 22.♖h3 ♕f5 23.♖e4 ♕xf4 24.♗xh7+ ♔f8 25.♗g6!
1-0, Campora-Koch, Izmir 2004.

Anish Giri @anishgiri · May 7
Why not? 😎

Indeed, a simple thumbs-up emoticon after 5.g4 👍 suffices as a reply to Anish Giri's 'Why not?' ∎

Nepo dominates Dortmund

Kramnik is often a danger to himself nowadays

Ian Nepomniachtchi is an extremely gifted player and when he is in form, playing his powerful chess at lightning speed, it's a scary thing to watch. In Dortmund, the 28-year-old Muscovite was on a roll, finishing a full point ahead of his closest pursuers. Vladimir 'Mr Dortmund' Kramnik fought like a lion, but took too many risks. **ERWIN L'AMI** reports.

Dortmund is probably not a destination I'd think of as a tourist. Although there are good restaurants in abundance, the city is fairly typical for the Ruhr region, which once was the heart of the German coal and steel industry. For chess fans, however, this is completely irrelevant, since Dortmund has been the home of an elite chess event for decades. This year, the Sparkassen Chess Meeting was held for the 46th time, and I travelled there with Anish Giri. It was Anish's

GEORGIOS SOULEIDIS

Tournament director Stefan Koth watches as Jenny Deppe, representing one of the sponsors, makes the first move in the key game in Round 5 between Ian Nepomniachtchi and 'Mr. Dortmund', Vladimir Kramnik. How 'Nepo' won you can read in his notes to that game at the end of this report.

Garry Kasparov famously noted in 1992: 'The most talented player here was Kramnik. The others make moves; he plays chess.'

second visit to Dortmund and my first.

For the past few years, the venue has been the NRW Orchestra Centre, where the audience is seated in spacious and comfortable seats with a clear view of the illuminated stage. Given the average age of the visitors, it is not uncommon to see some of them enjoying their seats a bit too much, falling asleep and starting to snore. What also caught my ear was the sound of something that is best described as stage-whispering in the playing hall. It turned out that every visitor was given

a headset to follow Klaus Bischoff's commentary. Apparently, again because of the above-mentioned average age of the visitors, some spectators needed to turn up the sound pretty loud. The players, however, from what I could see, seemed completely undisturbed and that, after all, is what matters. Speaking of the players, these days Dortmund has eight participants, which makes it a very fast event, despite the two rest days. With just seven rounds there is not much room for error!

'Mr. Dortmund' is Vladimir Kramnik, who made his debut here in 1992, when as a 16-year old he shared first in the Open tournament. Not only his win but particularly his play elicited historical praise from Garry Kasparov – the winner of the main tournament that year in his only appearance here – who famously noted: 'The most talented player here was Kramnik. The others make moves; he plays chess.'

Following his debut, Kramnik became a regular guest in the main event, and in the years since then, he has missed the tournament only twice! His fondness for Dortmund must have something to do with the fact that he has won it 10 times – or perhaps it's the other way around.

In recent years, however, Kramnik has failed to continue his reign in Dortmund. The last time he won was in 2011, and the past few years particularly have been less than generous for him.

Therefore, I was curious what the 'new' Kramnik would bring to Dortmund. If there have been the occasional moments in the past when he was criticized for not showing enough fighting spirit, these days he tends to draw attention to himself with too much fighting spirit. People just can't seem to make up their minds! His game in Round 2 is an example of the risks Kramnik is prepared to take these days.

Radoslaw Wojtaszek
Vladimir Kramnik
Dortmund 2018 (2)

position after 37...♔g7

A correct positional queen sacrifice has led to an endgame in which the d-pawn guarantees Black enough counterplay for a draw.
38.♕d4+ On the other hand, 38.♕xa6 ♖d6! would guarantee Black a win, since the checks run out after 39.♕b7 d2 40.♕b2+ f6 41.♕b7+ ♔f8 42.♕c8+ ♔e7 43.♕b7+ ♖d7 44.♕b4+ c5! 45.♕xc5+ ♔f7, and the d-pawn will decide.
38...♔g8 39.♕d8+

39...♔h7 That's the new Kramnik! Obviously, 39...♔g7 would have led to a handshake and a draw.
40.♕d4
Better was 40.♕f8! ♖f6 41.f3, threatening to bring the king in front of the d-pawn, while constraining Black on the kingside, when White is winning. The problem for Black is that he is unable to support his d-pawn, and attempting to do so with 41...♖f5 42.♕d6 ♖d5 loses to 43.♕xc6, when everything falls.
40...♖e2
Natural, because Black is trying to get his d-pawn forward, but wrong. 40...♔g8 or 40...♖e1 would have kept the balance. Now Wojtaszek gets a second chance, although perhaps this one is even more difficult to spot than the one on move 40.

In the foyer of the NRW Orchestra Centre, 32 local artists exhibited outdoor chess pieces that had been put in an artistic context or given an artistic twist. Here is a new suggestion how to protect your king.

41.♕d7
Instead, 41.♕f6! ♔g8 (or 41...d2 42.♕xf7+ ♔h8 43.♕b3 c5 44.♕d1!, followed by ♔f3, threatening ♕xe2, with a winning pawn ending) 42.♕xc6 d2 43.♕c2! would have done the job, although I can easily imagine that 43...♗c4!

ANALYSIS DIAGRAM

looks very scary here, when Black threatens 44...♗b3 45.♕xb3 ♖e1, promoting the d2-pawn. But 44.a6! gives White just enough time to regroup: 44...♗xa6 45.♔f3 ♗c4 46.♕d1, and Black has to give up the d2-pawn to avoid finding himself in a losing pawn ending.
41...♗c4 42.♕xc6 ♖c2 43.♕e4 ♖c3 44.♕d4 ♖c2 45.♕e4 ♖c3 46.♕d4 ♖c2 47.♕e4

Draw agreed. It was interesting to read in some reports that Wojtaszek had 'defended accurately' to 'hold the balance' after a 'strong queen sacrifice'. I think reality was somewhat different.

In the early rounds of the tournament, it was Jan-Krzysztof Duda who stood out. With daring play, not shying away from risks and complications, the 20-year-old Polish GM had climbed to the top of the rankings after three rounds. In Round 2, he defeated Liviu-Dieter Nisipeanu, who had an atrocious event, and in Round 3 he played his countryman Radoslaw Wojtaszek, who had won Dortmund the previous year. A nice rivalry, you could say, for the number one spot in their country, which Duda seems determined on winning.

Radek Wojtaszek vs. Jan-Krzysztof Duda, a clash between experience and youthful ambition. In Dortmund the determination of 20-year-old Duda prevailed.

Jan-Krzysztof Duda
Radoslaw Wojtaszek
Dortmund 2018 (3)
Trompowsky Attack

1.d4 ♘f6 2.♗g5
The Trompowsky remains a rare guest at top level, despite Carlsen using it in the first game of his World Championship match against Karjakin.
2...d5 3.♗xf6

3...gxf6
The most ambitious recapture, and as kids we were always taught to capture towards the centre! More common is 3...exf6 4.e3 ♗d6 5.♗d3 0-0, when Mamedyarov recently played a few blitz/rapid games with the set-up

♕f3, ♘d2, ♘e2, 0-0-0 (not necessarily in this order), followed by g4 and h4 with attack.
4.c4 dxc4 5.e3 c5 6.d5

> 'A nice rivalry, you could say, for the number one spot in their country, which Duda seems determined on winning.'

We are already in new territory, and with his last move Duda forced Wojtaszek into his first think. It's quite an achievement to get the Polish theoretician out of book on move 6! The game continuation is much more critical than 6.♗xc4 cxd4 7.exd4 ♗g7 8.♘c3 0-0, which had been seen in

a couple of games, but can only be better for Black.
Having said that, I don't think 6.d5 is going to revolutionize the line.

6...♗g7
Perhaps not the best move. Black has two interesting alternatives: 6...♕a5+ 7.♘c3 b5, for the moment holding on to the c-pawn, or the weird-looking 6...♖g8, with the same idea of keeping the c-pawn, as g2 is now hanging. After 7.g3 b5 8.a4 ♗b7!, Black would be able to exploit the weakening of the long diagonal.
7.♗xc4 f5 8.♘c3 ♘d7

always compensate for the pawn in the endgame.

9.♘ge2 I prefer 9.♘f3!?, to keep the black knight from e5, since 9...♘e5 10.♘xe5 ♗xe5 11.0-0 is strategically very dubious.

My computer insists that Black can play 9...a6 10.a4 ♕a5 11.0-0 ♘b6 12.♘d2 ♗d7 here, but it looks very artificial.

9...a6 10.a4 ♘e5 11. ♗a2 0-0
Minor inaccuracies over the past few moves have led to a position in which Black is already extremely comfortable.

12.0-0

12...♖b8
In fact, no preparation was needed, since 12...b5! 13.axb5 axb5 14.♘xb5 ♕b6 15.♘bc3 ♗a6! 16.♕d2 ♖fb8 would give Black an overwhelming position – indeed, the dream of every Benko-player!

13.♘g3 b5 14.axb5 axb5 15.♕c2 ♕d6
Preventing ♘xf5 by tactical means. Black could also have sacrificed the pawn with 15...c4 16.♘xf5 ♗xf5 17.♕xf5 ♕c8, with the idea that Black's queenside initiative will

16.♘ce2 16.♘xf5 ♘f3+! 17.gxf3 ♕g6+ 18.♔h1 ♗xf5 is Black's point.
16...b4
16...♖a8! 17.♘xf5 ♗xf5 18.♕xf5 ♕g6! is a beautiful idea, similar to the one mentioned on move 15. Only in this case, after 19.♕xg6 ♘xg6 20.♖fb1 c4! 21.♘c3 ♖a5!, followed by 21...♖fa8, White is losing the battle on the queenside.
17.♖ac1

17...b3
Based on a miscalculation. Despite Black having missed a few good options, even here 17...♗a6 18.♘xf5 ♕f6 was still a good and active possibility. For instance, 19.♘xg7 (19.♘f4 ♗xf1 20.♖xf1 ♘g6! protects against 21.♘h5 with 21...♕xb2!) 19...♕xg7 and 20...b3 is an annoying threat.
18.♗xb3 c4 19.♗xc4 ♖xb2 20.♕d1 ♕b4

Undoubtedly, this is what Radek had pinned his hopes on. And it does look good, because the bishop on c4 has nowhere to go.
21.♘d4! ♘xc4 22.♘c6
This sudden change of scenery forces Black to take some tough decisions.

22...♕c5

Missing White's reply. 22...♕b5 23.♘xe7+ ♔h8 24.♘xc8 ♖xc8 25.♘xf5 ♗f6 26.♕f3 ♕d7 was holding, but doesn't look very attractive.
However, 22...♘xe3 23.fxe3 ♕a3 24.♔h1!? is also not straightforward: 24...♔h8, and here 25.♘h5 also looks dangerous.

ANALYSIS DIAGRAM

My engine doesn't care much about appearances, though, and spits out 25...♗a6 26.♖a1 ♕d3 27.♕f3 ♗c4 28.♘xe7 ♕xf1+!! 29.♖xf1 ♗xf1 30.♕xf1 ♖fb8 31.♘xf5 ♖b1, with a drawn endgame.
23.♕a4! The key move that secures White's advantage. He is about to win back the knight.

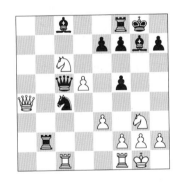

23...♖d2
Not the toughest defence.
A good defence was 23...♖b7 24.♕xc4 (24.♖xc4!? ♕xd5 25.♖d1 ♕e6 is worth considering as well, but with everything on one wing, I feel Black can have good hopes of holding) 24...♕xc4 25.♖xc4 ♖e8, when there is a lot of suffering ahead in the endgame. Still, I would be reluctant to say that Black is actually lost here.

23...♘b6 doesn't help much after 24.♖xc5 ♘xa4 25.♘xe7+, followed by 26.♖xc8.
24.♖xc4 ♕d6 25.♕a7 ♗f6

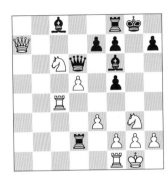

26.♘h5
26.e4! would have ended the game on the spot, since 26...f4 27.e5! ♗xe5 28.♘e4 haemorrhages material.
26...♔h8 27.♘xf6 exf6 28.♖d4

Black is completely lost. Duda finished off without any issues.
28...♖c2 29.♘b4 ♖c5 30.♖fd1 ♗d7 31.♕a6 ♕xa6 32.♘xa6 ♖b5 33.h4 ♖c8 34.♘b4 ♔g7 35.♔h2 ♔f8 36.♖1d2 ♖cb8 37.♘d3 ♔e7 38.♘f4 ♖b2 39.d6+ ♔f8 40.♘h5

Black resigned.

Vladislav Kovalev earned his ticket by winning the Aeroflot Open in Mosco
Often such qualifiers fall prey to the other participants, but not this time!

Overall, I felt that when faced with the two highest-rated players in the field, Vladimir Kramnik and Anish Giri, Duda still showed some vulnerability, but that may of course very well disappear in time. For now, he showed a very respectable +1 score, losing only to Kramnik.

While Kramnik probably has a standing invitation to play in Dortmund, most of the others are invited in the months leading up to the tournament. However, the first player to secure his spot for this edition was Vladislav Kovalev, the 24-year-old GM from Belarus, who earned his ticket by winning the Aeroflot Open in Moscow in February. It is not unusual for such qualifiers to fall prey to the other participants, but not this time! (The most famous exception to this rule was Victor Bologan, who won the Aeroflot Open in 2003 and then also Dortmund ahead of Kramnik and Anand!) Having already missed some very serious winning chances against Ian Nepomniachtchi in Round 2, Kovalev faced Anish Giri with the black pieces in Round 3.

Anish Giri
Vladislav Kovalev
Dortmund 2018 (3)

position after 34...♛e8

There isn't much happening here, because Black's 'weakness' on d5 isn't really a weakness. In an ideal world, White would exchange the queens and the dark-squared bishops, and put his king on d4 in order to try and win the bishop endgame, but in reality this is not going to happen. White decides to make some neutral moves first in order to reach move 40.

35.♛d1 Allowing a sudden tactic.
35...d4! 36.♛d2 Forced, since both 36.♗xd4 ♗xd4+ 37.♛xd4 ♛e1+ 38.♔h2 ♛e2! and 36.cxd4 ♛e3+ spell disaster. **36...dxc3 37.bxc3 ♛e6 38.♗d4 ♗xd4+ 39.cxd4 ♛a2 40.♛c3 ♛d5 41.♛d2 ♛a2 42.♛c3 h4 43.♔h1 a5 44.a4 ♛d5 45.♛d2 b6 46.f5 ♔g7 47.fxg6 fxg6 48.♗d1 ♛f5 49.♔g1 ♗d5 50.♗c2 ♛f6 51.♛e3 g5 52.♗d3 ♔h6 53.♗c2 ♔g7 54.♗d3 ♔h6 55.♗c2**
Kovalev has systematically improved his position to reach this diagram. What should Black play here?

55...♛f4! 56.♛d3 ♔g7!
Not fearing any ghosts. The king will be brought over to the queenside.
57.♛g6+ ♔f8 58.♛d3 ♔g7 59.♛g6+ ♔f8 60.♛d3 ♔e7 61.♗d1 ♛e4 62.♛d2

Any bishop endgame is hopeless, with all White's pawns fixed on light squares.
62...♔d6 63.♗c2 ♛f4 64.♛d3 ♔c7 65.♛h7+ ♔b8 66.♛d3 g4!

The finishing touch. White can't let this pawn pass to g3, but taking it costs the g2-pawn.

67.hxg4 ♛xg4 68.♛g6 ♛xd4+ 69.♔h1 ♗b7 70.♛e8+ ♔a7 71.♗f5 ♛d1+ 72.♔h2 ♛d6+ 73.♔h1 ♛g3

And White resigned. Ruthless play by Kovalev.

In the end, Kovalev scored +1, like Duda, without losing a single game, but it should be noted that he was also winning against Vladimir Kramnik in the final round! Truly an excellent debut at the highest level.

As already hinted, it was not to be Vladimir Kramnik's tournament. Here's the game the Russian legend lost in Round 6 to Anish Giri, with the latter's comments.

NOTES BY
Anish Giri

Vladimir Kramnik
Anish Giri
Dortmund 2018 (6)
Queen's Pawn Opening

I am not particularly proud of this game, nor is it my most interesting game from the tournament. Still, I am yet to be spoilt to the point when I will refuse to annotate a win against Vladimir Kramnik with the black pieces, in a tournament as prestigious as the Dortmund one.

1.♘f3 d5 2.e3
While I was helping Vladimir for

'Now that Kramnik has got rid of me, I wasn't too surprised to see that he got back to his old favourite opening system.'

the Candidates Tournament in Berlin earlier this year, I did everything within my power to stop him from going for this rather innocent opening system, which he has used way too often in the last couple of years. Now that he has got rid of me, I wasn't too surprised to see that he got back to his old favourite.

2...♘f6 3.d4 c5 4.♘bd2 e6 5.b3 cxd4 6.exd4 ♗b4!?

An idea of my coach Vladimir Chuchelov, who had decided that the 1.d4 2.♘f3 3.e3 system had been around for far too long. Black obviously is fine just finishing his development, but this impatient attempt seems to work as well.

7.♗b2 ♘e4 8.♗d3 ♘c6 9.0-0
9.♗xe4 dxe4 10.♘e5 is another critical junction, but the magic button was pressed here, too.

9...♗c3!

The point of Black's play. I would never dare to trap my knight on

c3 without triple checking that it sits comfortably there.

10.♗xc3 ♘xc3 11.♛e1
11.♛c1 ♘b4 is similar, but different. (11...♛f6!? is an extra option that probably made my opponent go for the other queen move.)

11...♘b4

12.♘b1 This is not very principled, and I must say I was somewhat surprised to see it. I was assuming that Vladimir was going to try to prove me wrong, but knowing that he was up against preparation, he decided to simplify and get rid of my knight on c3, which is both my pride and sorrow.

Moves like 12.a4!? or, let's say, 12.♘e5, 12.♛e3 are more critical, but White runs significant risk as well.

If I manage to cement my c3-knight, he will regret what he has done. The backward c2-pawn will remain forever a target and so will the unsupported d4-pawn.

12...♘xd3 13.♛xc3 ♘f4 14.♛e3 ♘g6 15.c4 dxc4 16.bxc4 0-0

Here I believe Black should be very comfortable, but I expected White to eventually go for a4-a5, and it is easy to imagine how the game will simplify further. Vladimir started surprising me somewhat.

17.♘c3 17.♘bd2, followed by a4, was what I had expected. Funnily enough, in the 11.♕c1 ♘b4 variation we would get the same position with a tempo up for White, but as I already mentioned, Vladimir probably disliked 11...♕f6 there, since he would have had to sacrifice a pawn, with unclear consequences.

17...♗d7
Aimed against d5 ideas. I didn't want my bishop staring at the d5-pawn.
I could also have simply gone 17...b6! 18.♖fd1 ♗b7, when after 19.d5 exd5 20.cxd5 ♖e8 21.♕d4 ♖c8, White is simply worse, since his c3-knight is hanging in the air, unable to support the d5-pawn in the long run.

18.♖fd1 ♖c8

19.♘d2 I had expected 19.c5, when I didn't think I was really playing for an advantage with the backward pawn on b7, but I can imagine that Vladimir didn't want to let me have the d5-square.

19...♘h4 I was spoilt for choice here, so I just picked one of the many moves that I considered normal. I thought it made some sense to go for a set-up with ...♘f5, ...♕c7, ...♖fd8 and see what happens.

20.♕d3 ♘f5 21.♖ac1
This move I hadn't expected either. I kept waiting for a4 to appear. It is something I would do, trying to get rid of a potential weakness; but

Vladimir wanted to create play of his own.

21...♕c7 22.d5 ♖fd8

I was very satisfied with my position here. White's 'breakthrough' with d5 (which made me think of the famous book by Damsky with the same title) really didn't yield him anything at all this time. Still, I didn't think that I was already really better.

23.h3
I had expected 23.♘f3 first, but then, when I saw that after 23...♕xc4 White has no way to punish me for the shaky coordination and the pinned bishop on the d-file, I realized that Vladimir would probably start with 23.h3 to try and get a better version of this endgame. It would have been more ambitious of me not to aim for the queen trade on c4, but I got obsessed by the little tactics in the ensuing endgame and wanted to test my calculations against those of my opponent.
After 23.♘f3 ♕xc4 24.♕xc4 ♖xc4 25.dxe6 (25.♘e5 ♖cc8! 26.dxe6 ♗xe6) 25...fxe6 26.♘e5 (26.♖d3 e5!?) 26...♖d4! 27.g4 ♗a4! 28.♖xd4 ♘xd4!

is a very nice geometry that got me

excited about the ...♕xc4 endings.

23...b6

23...h6!? was more ambitious, and it was only on the next move that I realized it could have been cleverer: 24.♘f3 ♘d6! (24...♕xc4 would be possible too). Now there is no ♘g5, although White keeps some play after 25.♘e4!?

ANALYSIS DIAGRAM

when the computer points out the strong sequence 25...♘xc4!? 26.d6 ♕c6 27.♕d4!? ♕b5! 28.♖b1 ♕f5! 29.♘g3 ♕c5! 30.♕xc5 ♖xc5 31.♖xb7 ♗c6 32.♖xa7 ♖xd6 33.♖xd6 ♘xd6, with a drawish endgame that the engine judges to be slightly in Black's favour.

24.♘f3

Here I realized that the endgame is probably just a draw, and that I might actually be doing very well here in general. But then, when weighing my options, I failed to find an ideal way of dealing with White's ideas, so in the end, I decided to go for the endgame anyway.

24...♕xc4

After 24...h6, 25.d6 bothered me quite a bit, since my f5-knight has no

Anish Giri wasn't particularly proud of his game against Kramnik. 'Still, I am yet to be spoilt to the point when I will refuse to annotate a win against Vladimir Kramnik with the black pieces in Dortmund.'

squares. It seems that after 25...♕b7! 26.♘e5 the position is roughly equal, despite being very complicated. After 24...♗e8 I also got thrown off by 25.g4, when the simple 25...♘e7! was actually playable and quite strong, since White has to find 26.♕e3! to maintain the balance.

25.♕xc4

After 25.dxe6 Black has 25...♕xe6!.

25...♖xc4 26.dxe6

Inverting the move order is not possible: 26.♘e5 ♖cc8!.

26...fxe6

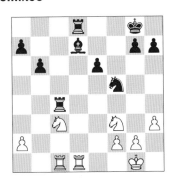

27.♖d3

I had noticed this move right before playing 24...♕xc4 and it alarmed me somewhat at first, but then I noticed I had some tactical resources here. After 27.♘e5 ♖d4 28.♘e2 there is also 28...♖d6, besides 28...♖d5. Both lead to simplifications in which White regains the pawn and the game should end in a draw. (After 28.g4, 28...♗a4! still works.)

27...e5!

27...♖c5 28.♖cd1 h6 is another way to

When Vladimir played this slightly strange move, I realized that he was in the mood for some adventures, despite the fact that the game should actually

hold, but the text-move is obviously a lot nicer.

28.♘xe5

After 28.♖cd1 there are two ways for Black:

– 28...♖e8 29.♖xd7 ♖xc3 30.♖xa7 e4, and the backward e6-pawn has turned into a swan on e4 that will seal the deal.

– The ambitious one, which I liked, was 28...♘d4!? 29.♘xe5 ♗f5 30.♘xc4 ♗xd3 31.♖xd3 ♘e2+ 32.♘xe2 ♖xd3. I felt that this endgame could only be dangerous for White, given his shaky coordination. But he has 33.♘e3!, after which it seems to be objectively equal.

28...♖d4 29.♖f3

come to an end soon. I had more time and a comfortably equal endgame, so I didn't mind waiting to see what he would come up with.

29...♘h4 30.♖e3 ♘f5

I didn't think this was a particularly good move, but I just wanted confirmation that Vladimir wanted to play on. In fact, I had every right to play on here as well, with any move, let's say 30...♗e8 or 30...♖c8, but as so often, the player who wants to push is the one to over-push.

31.♖ee1 ♗e8 32.♘e4

The white knights are pretty in the centre, but I didn't really mind. The queens are off and I didn't really see from which angle I was going to be attacked.

32...♖a4 33.♖c7!? ♖xa2

I realized that this could be my chance, since White was low on time and sacrificed a pawn, rather adventurously. Before I could get second thoughts, I decided to take the gift immediately.

34.♔h2

White has no extra resources to bring to the table, so this move, which is typically nasty with the queens on, didn't impress me. In fact, I was happy to get time for ...h6, after which I have even fewer ghosts to fear.

34.♘f3! was the only way to ask Black some questions, since g4 is a serious threat: 34...♖a3!. Not the only move, but the most natural one and the best attempt to prevent g4. 35.♘eg5 Renewing the g4 threat. Now there is a forced line: 35...h6 (35...♖ad3 is another way to maintain the balance) 36.♘e6 ♖d7 37.♘c8 ♘d6 (37...♖e7? 38.♘c7!) 38.♘ed4!, and here computer points out that it is clever to start with 38...♖a5!, gaining a tempo in the complicated position after 39.♖exe8+ ♘xe8 40.♖xe8+ ♔f7

ANALYSIS DIAGRAM

when I guess Black is in no danger of losing, although the computer claims White should also be fine. True, his knights are well coordinated and I will probably get no time to push my pawns, while being harassed with all sorts of forks and checks.

34.♘g4, threatening ♘f6+ and a perpetual, would most likely lead to a draw after 34...♗g6 35.♘e5!.

34...h6 35.♘g4?!

35.♘f3! was already the only move to hold the balance: 35...♖a3 36.♘g3!, and as the rook will enter the 7th rank, White gets enough play: 36...♘xg3 37.fxg3 ♔f8 38.♖ee7 ♖ad3 39.♘e5 ♖3d5 40.♖xa7, with dynamic equality.

35...♔f8!

Obviously, I was not going to allow a perpetual now that there were absolutely no threats to my king and the connected passers on the queenside were waiting for their moment. Finally we have entered ∓ terri-

tory, because White had wasted his chances to create concrete threats and Black has fully consolidated.

36.♖ec1?

Going back with 36.♘e5 was called for.

36...♖e2 37.f3

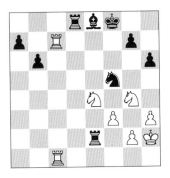

37...♘h4?

Now that I had more time, more pawns and no more worries, I wanted to take over the 'initiative' as well, but in fact it would have been far stronger to start pushing the pawns. I had actually missed the 39.♔g1! resource and was also seduced by the pretty mate after 38.♔g3, which Vladimir, by the way, confessed he had almost walked into...

After 37...a5! Black is already winning. 37...♘d4!? was another very strong idea.

38.♘gf2

38.♔g3 invites 38...♖xg2+ 39.♔xh4 ♖d5!, followed by ...♖h5 or ...g5, mate.

38...♗g6

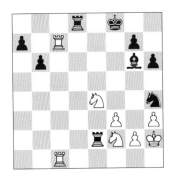

39.♖c8?

39.♔g1! was the move we had both missed (I had expected 39.♔g3, when I planned to reroute the knight with tempo to e3 or d4, as in the game): 39...♗xe4 (39...a5 40.♖a7, and White apparently generates just enough play for equality with ♖cc7) 40.fxe4 ♔g8 41.♖xa7 ♖f8 42.♖f1 ♖f6. This would be a nice ∓ to finish the day with, but if I had known that I had blown away a win in time-trouble, I wouldn't have been too happy.

39...♖e8!

Now I am back in the driver's seat, and I was very satisfied with how I conducted the technical phase of the game.

40.♔g3 ♘f5+ 41.♔h2 ♘d4!

'It is remarkable that it was still possible to mess it up completely, and with the most natural move, no less.'

Threatening all sorts of nasty ...♘xf3+, ...♗xe4 things and introducing ♔g3 ♖xe4 ideas.

42.♖1c3

After, for example, 42.♔g3 I liked the simplifying 42...♖2xe4!? 43.fxe4 ♘e2+ 44.♔f3 ♘xc1 45.♖xc1, and Black should win easily by pushing the pawns. I was even considering 45...a5!? 46.♖c6 ♗f7 47.♖xb6 ♖a8, with a trivial win as confirmed by the comp.

42...a5!

A strong move to underline that White has absolutely no moves here.

43.♖8c4 ♖d8 44.♖c7 ♘e6!?

The most controlled way to win the game. I could also have calculated some brutal pawn push, but I didn't want to allow any counterplay with two rooks on the 7th rank, which could lead to a study-like escape in some of the variations I had envisioned.

45.♖7c6 ♘f4 46.♖c8

After 46.♔g3 I had calculated a long forced line with 46...♖xe4 47.♘xe4 ♘e2+ 48.♔f2 ♗xe4! 49.♖c8! ♘xc3 50.♖xd8+ ♔e7 51.♖c8! ♘d1+!

52.♔e2 ♗f5!, and Black seems to be winning. In fact, 46...♘h5+!, with the idea of taking on e4 with the bishop after ♔h2, would have been a lot simpler.

46...♖e8!

The cleanest solution. The same motif as on move 39, except that now my knight is better positioned and my pawn is already on a5.

47.♖xe8+ ♔xe8 48.♖c8+ ♔d7 49.♖g8 ♘e6!?

Running with the pawns would win as well at this point, but this leaves White no hope.

50.♔g3 ♔c7!?

This is just enjoying it too much, because White doesn't even get to give a check anymore.

51.h4 ♖c2!

White is unable to organize any sort of counterplay, and it is incredible how winning Black is at this point.

52.♖a8

Allowing me to demonstrate my idea to the full.

52...♔b7 53.♖h8 ♖c6!

Continuing the no-check policy. The rest was already fairly unnecessary.

54.h5 ♗xe4 55.♘xe4 a4 56.♖e8 a3 57.♖e7+ ♔a6 58.♖e8 ♔a7 59.♘d2 a2 60.♘b3 ♖c3 61.♘a1 ♖c1 62.♖xe6 ♖xa1 63.♖e2 b5 64.♔f4

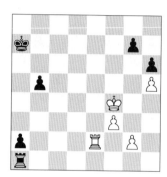

It is remarkable that it was still possible to mess it up completely, and with the most natural move, no less.

64...♔b6

And not 64...b4?? 65.♖b2!, with a study-like draw. Incredible! But after the text-move White resigned.

∎ ∎ ∎

His third-round loss against Kovalev was a big blow for Anish, but he took it well and bounced back with wins against Nisipeanu and Kramnik. In the final round, he even had some chances to fight for first place when he got a winning position against Duda. Alas, it was not to be, because he let Duda off the hook, while his direct rival Nepomniachtchi did what he had to do – win his own game against Georg Meier.

Going into the last round half a point ahead of the field, some would play conservatively and others would not!

The cast of the 46th Dortmund tournament with dignitaries and officials. Gerd Kolbe (Event Director), NN, Jan-Krzysztof Duda, Vladislav Kovalev, Georg Meier, NN, Radek Wojtaszek, Stefan Koth (Tournament Director), Vladimir Kramnik, Ian Nepomniachtchi, Liviu-Dieter Nisipeanu and Anish Giri.

Ian Nepomniachtchi
Georg Meier
Dortmund 2018 (7)
French Defence, Rubinstein Variation

1.e4 e6 2.d4 d5 3.♘c3 dxe4 4.♘xe4 ♘d7 5.♘f3 ♘gf6 6.♘xf6+ ♘xf6 7.♘e5

7...♗d6

I am no expert here, but 7...♘d7 8.♗f4 ♘xe5 9.♗xe5, as played by Georg Meier in a couple of online blitz games, and now 9...♗d7 (...♗c6 with ...♕d7 and ...0-0-0 coming) looks very reasonable for Black.

8.♗g5

8.♕f3 c5 9.♗b5+ ♔e7 10.0-0 cxd4 11.♗f4 gave White great compensa-tion in Dominguez-Meier, chess.com blitz 2018, but I think 8...0-0 9.♗g5 h6 10.♗h4 ♗e7, with ...♕d5 coming, should fix this issue.

8...h6 9.♗h4 0-0 10.♗d3 c5 11.♕e2

11...♕a5+

All played very fast by Ian Nepom-niachtchi, who praised his second Vladimir Potkin for showing him the details of this line. Georg was on his own now in this already very dangerous-looking position.

Instead of the check, 11...cxd4 was the alternative, when White must choose where to castle: 12.0-0-0 (12.0-0 ♗e7! may not be so bad for Black) 12...♕c7 (12...♗e7 13.g4!) 13.♗xf6 gxf6

14.♘f3. But this is very dangerous. White has this typical slow attack with h4 and g4, and there is very little Black can do to oppose that plan. A sample line is 14...♖d8 15.♔b1 ♗e7 16.h4 ♕f4 17.g4 e5 18.♖hg1 ♔f8 19.♘e1!, with the idea to regroup with ♗e4 and ♘d3.

12.c3 cxd4 13.♘c4

13...♕c5

I was about to write that 13...♕d5, with the idea that after 14.♗xf6 gxf6 15.♕g4+ ♔h8 White can no longer take on d4 with tempo, was a better move, but that wouldn't promise equality either in view of 14.♗xf6 gxf6 15.♗e4 ♕c5 16.♘xd6 ♕xd6 17.♖d1.

ANALYSIS DIAGRAM

but here the line continues 17...e5 18.♕h5 f5! 19.♗xf5 ♗xf5 20.♕xf5 ♕g6! 21.♕xg6+ fxg6 22.cxd4 exd4, and because 23.♖xd4 ♖ae8+! 24.♔f1 ♖c8 is even dangerous for White, the position after move 22 is just equal.

14.♗xf6 gxf6 15.♕g4+ ♔h8 16.cxd4!

The big difference with 13...♕d5.

16...♕b4+ 17.♔f1

It was also possible to take the positional route with 17.♔e2 ♗c7 18.♖ac1 (18.♕e4!?) 18...♖g8 19.♕h4 ♔g7 20.♖hd1 ♗d7 21.♔f1, when White should be much better. Ian, however, was out for mate.

17...♗c7 18.♕e4 f5

19.♕h4

Ian Nepomniachtchi rounded off with a flashy last-round win against Georg Meier to finish a full point ahead the best of the rest.

This looks very strong and works out splendidly in the game.

Another violent attempt to get at the black king is 19.♕e3 ♔g7 20.g4!, when Black should try to hold on with 20...f4 21.♕e4 ♗d7!, not fearing any checks on h7. The position is less clear than it looks.

19...♔g7

I can't possibly give this move a question mark, since the right sequence of moves is impossible to find.

Brace yourself: 19...♔h7 20.g4 b5! 21.g5, and now 21...bxc4 22.♕xh6+ ♔g8 23.g6 leads to a quick mate, but 21...♗f4!!

ANALYSIS DIAGRAM

stops the move g5-g6 after ♕xh6, and that suddenly stops White's attack. Best now is 22.♕xf4 bxc4 23.♕h4 ♕d2! 24.♕xh6+ ♔g8, when it is the queen that stops the g5-g6 break, and Black is ready to start counterplay with ...♖b8xb2 or ...♗b7.

I should mention that 21...♖h8 is also an excellent practical try, but White should be on top after 22.♖g1 h5 23.g6+! fxg6 24.♗e2! (threatening ♗xh5) 24...♗d8 25.♕g3 g5 26.♘e5 ♗b7 27.♘f7 ♕e7 28.♘xh8 (28.♗xh5!?) 28...g4. Still, the position is very messy.

20.g4

20...f4

Here 20...b5 21.gxf5 bxc4 22.f6+ leads to mate, but with the black king on h7, Black would now take on d3.

21.♖g1 ♗d7

22.♕h5!

22.g5 h5! is a last pitfall to avoid. After the game continuation it's all very clear-cut.

22...♖h8 23.g5 hxg5 24.♕xg5+ ♔f8 25.♕f6 ♖xh2 26.♖g7 ♗e8

Or 26...♕e7 27.♖g8+!.

27.♗h7

And Black resigned, because mate is imminent.

■ ■ ■

Vintage 'Nepo', and a great way to claim a well-deserved tournament victory. Ian Nepomniachtchi is an extremely gifted player, and when he is in form, playing his powerful chess at lightning speed, it's a scary thing to watch! He was always around the top of the leader-board and when he accelerated towards the end, nobody could keep pace. We finish this report with another characteristic win by the tournament winner, against his countryman, with his own notes.

NOTES BY
Ian Nepomniachtchi

Ian Nepomniachtchi
Vladimir Kramnik
Dortmund 2018 (5)
Ruy Lopez, Møller Defence

1.e4 e5 2.♘f3 ♘c6 3.♗b5 a6
A surprise. Usually Vladimir Borisovich chooses the Berlin Variation.
4.♗a4 ♘f6 5.0-0

5...♗c5 Taking into account the subsequent development of events, it can be assumed that the more customary move order – 5...b5 6.♗b3 ♗c5 7.a4 does not allow Black to adopt the idea 7...b4 on account of 8.♘xe5 ♘xe5 9.d4 ♗xd4 10.♕xd4, when the white bishop does not have to fear the ...c5-c4 advance.

6.c3 b5 This year Wojtaszek against Topalov and Carlsen against Karjakin played 6...0-0 7.d4 ♗a7, although this variation has the reputation of being not the most reliable.

7.♗b3 7.♗c2 d5 leads to very sharp and irrational variations, which, as far as I know, have been analysed almost to a draw.

7...d6 8.a4 b4!?

This move was a revelation to me. Black allows a blow in the centre in not the most successful version: now in some variations the b4-pawn is hanging.

Other moves occur far more often: 8...♖b8, 8...♗g4 or 8...♗b7.

9.d4 ♗a7

10.♗g5
The exchange of queens looks tempting, but in the endgame Black obtains counterplay thanks to his active pieces and the opening of the b-file: 10.dxe5 ♘xe5 11.♘xe5 dxe5 12.♕xd8+ ♔xd8 13.♘d2 (13.♗xf7 ♖f8 14.♗d5 ♘xd5 15.exd5 a5 16.♗e3 ♗xe3 17.fxe3 ♖xf1+ 18.♔xf1 bxc3 with equality) 13...♔e7 14.cxb4 ♗e6 15.♗xe6 ♔xe6 16.b3 ♗d4 17.♖a2 c5 18.bxc5 ♗xc5, and after the activation of his rooks Black should be able to equalize.

The immediate 10.♗d5 does not look very convincing: 10...♘xd5 11.exd5 ♘e7 12.dxe5 dxe5 13.♘xe5 ♕xd5 14.♕xd5 ♘xd5 15.♘c6 bxc3 16.♖d1 ♗e6 17.♘xc3 ♘xc3 18.bxc3 ♗c5 19.♗f4 0-0 with a level position.

10...♖b8

11.♗d5

As before, no advantage is promised by 11.dxe5 ♘xe5 12.♘xe5 dxe5 13.♕xd8+ ♔xd8 14.♗xf7 bxc3 15.♘xc3 (15.bxc3 ♖f8, with obvious compensation for the pawn) 15...♖xb2 16.♘d5 ♗d4!? 17.♖ad1 (17.♘xf6 h6! 18.♗h4 g5 19.♗g3 ♖f8 20.♖ab1 ♖xb1 21.♖xb1 ♖xf7 22.♖d1 ♗d7, and already White must think about equalizing) 17...h6 18.♗c1 ♖b8.

At the board the following line seemed interesting: 11.a5!? 0-0 12.♗a4 ♘e7 13.♘bd2 (13.♗xf6 gxf6 14.♘bd2 ♘g6 and despite his spoiled pawn structure, here Black has a fully equal game) 13...♘g6 14.h3. Here it is probably easier playing White, but there is still all to play for.

11...♘e7

12.dxe5

Captivated by the e5-pawn, I missed a worthy positional alternative: 12.♗xf6 gxf6 13.♗c4 ♘g6 14.♘bd2 0-0 15.a5 with comfortable play. But even here, for example after 15...f5 16.dxe5 dxe5 17.♕c2 ♔h8!?, Black has numerous interesting ideas.

12...♘fxd5 13.exd5 0-0

13...dxe5? is bad because of 14.♘xe5.

14.exd6 ♕xd6 15.c4 ♘f5

It should be mentioned that, by instantly performing all his opening moves, Kramnik had already accumulated several bonus minutes, so that if only from these considerations I did not harbour any great illusions regarding my position. The pawn centre is extremely unstable, and nearly all the black pieces are already in play.

16.♘bd2

A simple and sensible move. White completes his development. The computer recommends 16.♕c1!? f6 17.♗f4 ♕d7 18.♘bd2 g5 19.♗g3, and now both 19...h5 20.♘e4 ♕g7 21.d6 h4 22.dxc7 ♖b6 23.c5 ♖e6 and 19...g4 20.♘h4 ♘xg3 21.hxg3 f5 require a detailed analysis.

16...f6

Of course, not 16...h6? 17.♘e4 ♕g6 18.♘e5 and White wins.

17.♗h4

A critical moment. Black is now at a crossroads: he can immediately regain the pawn, retaining the advantage of the two bishops; he can undermine the centre while the white pieces are insufficiently well coordinated; or he can simply complete his development with the most natural moves.

17...♕f4?!

Kramnik follows the first course. Let us consider all the possibilities in order.

A) 17...g5. During the game this moved seemed to me to be rather committing. Now Black cannot attack the g2-pawn, and indeed, why play this when it is possible to regain the material without any

weakening? Nevertheless, the idea of ...g5-g4 enriches his arsenal: 18.♗g3 ♘xg3 19.hxg3 ♕xg3 20.c5 ♕f4 21.♘b3 ♗b7 22.♘a5 ♖a8. Not all are promised a bright future, but at least one of the bishops breaks free. For example, 23.♘d4 ♗xd5 24.♘dc6 ♖bd8, and now:

ANALYSIS DIAGRAM

A1) 25.♘xa7 (both knights on the edge of the board – this is very risky) 25...♗xg2 26.♕b3+ ♗d5 27.♕g3 ♕e4 28.♔h2 ♖de8 29.♖ae1 ♕xe1 30.♖xe1 ♖xe1.

ANALYSIS DIAGRAM

This looks horrifying for White, but the computer holds the draw;

A2) 25.♘e7+ ♔h8 26.♘xd5 ♕e4 27.♘xf6 ♕f5 28.♕e1 ♖xf6 29.♖c1 g4 with attacking chances;

A3) 25.♘xd8 ♖xd8 26.♖c1 ♕e4 27.f3 ♕e3+ 28.♔h2 g4 29.fxg4 ♕h6+ 30.♔g1 ♕e3+ with equality.

B) 17...c6. A forceful move. With accurate play the position quickly becomes lifeless. 18.♖c1 (it looks very presumptuous to play 18.dxc6 ♕xc6: the resulting position is a vivid example of the advantage of the

two bishops) 18...cxd5 19.♘b3! dxc4
20.♕xd6 ♘xd6 21.♗g3

ANALYSIS DIAGRAM

21...♖d8 22.♘a5 ♖a8 23.♘c6 ♖d7
24.♘xa7 ♖axa7 25.♗xd6 ♖xd6
26.♖xc4 ♗d7 27.♖xb4 a5 28.♖b8+
♔f7 29.b3 ♖d3 with the idea of
...♗e6. The variation is quite logical
and to some extent forced.

C) 17...♗d7 and 17...♖e8. In my
view too slow, although these moves
do not spoil anything. White's
plan remains the same – rook to c1,
knights if possible to b3 and d4, and
exchange the bishop on g3. Complicated, double-edged play with
roughly equal chances.

18.♗g3 ♘xg3 19.hxg3 ♕xg3

20.c5! A key idea, on which White's
conception rests. The rampant bishop
is brought to order.
20...♕g6
After 20...♕f4 21.♖c1 Black very
much lacks the pawn on g5.
21.♖c1
Initially we both assessed this
position as roughly equal. Vladimir
Borisovich was obviously counting
on his formidable bishops, whereas
I was entertaining hopes of main-

On the final day, Arkady Dvorkovich, former Russian deputy prime minister and a passionate chess lover, visited Dortmund to promote his candidacy for FIDE President in the upcoming elections.

taining my hanging pawns. But the
longer I studied the situation on the
board, the more attractive White's
prospects seemed to be, and the more
firm my hopes became. It proved
not so easy to discover a satisfactory
response for Black, even in analysis.

21...♕f7 A very solid move, but now
Black switches to defence. To retain
the former activity of the queen does
not prove possible.
21...♖d8? 22.d6 cxd6 23.c6 is
completely bad.
The reckless 21...b3 also does not
promise an easy life: 22.♘xb3 ♗h3
(22...♖b4 23.♘bd4 ♗h3 24.♘h4 ♕g5
25.♘df3 and White wins; sleight
of hand, so to speak) 23.♘h4 ♕g5

24.♖c3! with a clear white advantage.
And after 21...♗h3 22.♘h4 ♕g4
23.♖c4 ♕xd1 24.♖xd1 ♗c8 25.♘b3 it
becomes clear that even the exchange
of queens does nothing to simplify
the problem: 25...c6 26.d6 ♗e6
27.♖dc1, and only a miracle enables
Black to defend.
22.♘e4
22.♘b3 appealed to me less, since in
the variation 22...♗b7 23.c6 ♗c8 the
d5-d6 idea clearly loses in strength.

22...♖e8?!
The b3-square has remained vacant
for the queen, which may prove
useful in the following important
variation: 22...♗g4 23.♕b3 ♖fe8
24.♖fe1. Now Black can resist with

24...h6! (after 24...♖bd8 25.♘d4 the versatile cavalry creates too many threats, and the white pawns remain immune) 25.♘d4 f5 26.♘d2 ♖xe1+ 27.♖xe1 ♗xc5 28.♘e6 ♗d6 29.♘c4 f4 30.♘xd6 cxd6 31.a5 ♕f6 32.♕c2. White retains some initiative, but with due accuracy Black should be able to hold the position.

23.♖e1 ♗f5

In this version 23...♗g4 is less good: 24.♕d3! ♖bd8 25.♘fd2 ♗c8 26.d6 cxd6 27.cxd6, with appreciable pressure. It is staggering, but the move 22...♖e8 proved to be a serious inaccuracy.

24.♘g3 ♖xe1+ 24...♗g4 25.♕d3 is excellent for White.

25.♕xe1 ♗g4

After 25...♕xd5? 26.♘xf5 ♕xf5 27.♕e7 Black is helpless. White's advantage is also undisputed in the event of other bishop moves, for example 25...♗g6 26.d6 cxd6 27.cxd6 ♗b6 28.♘h4 ♕d5 29.♖d1 ♕e5 30.♕xe5 fxe5 31.♘xg6 hxg6 32.b3.

26.♕e4

It is time to take stock. White has succeeded in maintaining his centre and arranging his pieces well. After the exchange of a pair of rooks the back rank becomes a real weakness, and the d5-d6 break becomes an extremely annoying threat.

26...h5 27.♘f5

27.♘h4, with the same ideas, was even stronger.

27...♖e8

27...♗xf5 28.♕xf5 ♖d8 29.d6 cxd6 30.cxd6 g6 31.♕d3 ♗b8 32.♖c6 a5 33.♘d2 and White is winning.

28.♕d3

28...♗b8

I don't know whether this move deserves a question mark, but, in defending against d5-d6, Black is really too pitiless to his once formidable dark-squared bishop. 28...♗d7 29.♘3h4 ♖e5 30.♘e3, and White suppresses the opponent's attempts to develop activity.

29.♘3h4 ♗e2

For want of something better, Black dislodges the queen from its optimal square.

30.♕d2 ♗g4

White wins after 30...a5 31.d6 cxd6 32.cxd6.

31.♘e3?

Of course I saw 31.♕xb4, but I was too engrossed in manoeuvring and

I did not want to change the character of the position. Although in view of the variation 31...♕xd5 32.♕xb8 ♕e6 33.♕xc7 ♗xf5 34.♘xf5 ♕xf5, I should definitely not have avoided the obvious pawn capture: 35.c6 ♖e2 36.♕b6 with an easy win.

31...♗d7?

31...f5! could have significantly complicated White's task. After the accurate 32.g3 ♗a7 33.♖c4 the lion's share of the advantage is retained, but there is no longer a mechanical win.

32.♕xb4 a5

32...f5 loses to 33.c6.

33.♕xa5 c6 34.d6 ♕b3 35.♕c3 ♕xa4 36.♘hf5 ♕e4 37.♘e7+ ♔h8 38.♕b3 ♖f8

39.♕c2 To be on the safe side, White exchanges the queens.

39...♕xc2 40.♘xc2 ♔h7 41.♘d4 Black resigned.

A very complicated game. The main events in it occurred during a comparatively short stretch – from the 15th to the 23rd moves – but the nuances of the confrontation between a couple of agile knights and two powerful bishops are disclosed only in analysis. ∎

Dortmund 2018				1	2	3	4	5	6	7	8		cat. XIX TPR
1 Ian Nepomniachtchi	IGM	RUS	2757	*	½	½	½	1	1	½	1	5	2868
2 Anish Giri	IGM	NED	2782	½	*	0	½	½	1	½	1	4	2758
3 Vladislav Kovalev	IGM	BLR	2655	½	1	*	½	½	½	½	½	4	2776
4 Jan-Krzysztof Duda	IGM	POL	2737	½	½	½	*	½	0	1	1	4	2764
5 Georg Meier	IGM	GER	2628	0	½	½	½	*	½	½	1	3½	2733
6 Vladimir Kramnik	IGM	RUS	2792	0	0	½	1	½	*	½	½	3	2662
7 Radoslaw Wojtaszek	IGM	POL	2733	½	½	½	0	½	½	*	½	3	2671
8 Liviu-Dieter Nisipeanu	IGM	GER	2672	0	0	½	0	0	½	½	*	1½	2510

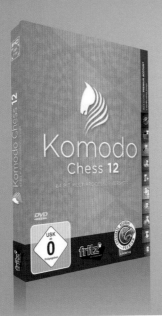

Capa's bishop sac

This classic sac exposes the enemy king. The eternal question remains: will the initiative prove worth the material?

wo years ago the following miniature was played in the French Team Championship.

Vladimir Hamitevici
Sebastien Cossin
Drancy 2016
1.b3 e5 2.♗b2 ♘c6 3.c4 ♘f6 4.e3 d5 5.cxd5 ♘xd5 6.d3 ♗c5 7.a3 0-0 8.b4

After White's many pawn moves Black is clearly ahead in development, and he decided to take his chance here:
8...♗xe3! 9.fxe3 ♘xe3 10.♕d2 ♘d4! An important idea in the follow-up of the piece sac. Black threatens to win back more material. Now after
11.♗xd4 exd4
White's king was stuck in the middle, and Black's octopus untouchable.

12.♘f3 ♗g4 13.h4 Already a desperate move, but a proper defence is not to be seen, e.g. 13.♔f2 ♗xf3 14.gxf3 ♕h4+ 15.♔g1 ♖ae8, with the rook heading to g6. The knock-out soon followed. **13... a5 14.b5 ♗xf3 15.gxf3 ♖e8 16.♗e2 ♖e6 17.♔f2 ♕d6 18.h5 ♖ae8 19.♖a2 ♖e5 20.♖h3 ♖g5 21.♗f1 ♕e6 22.♖h4 ♘d1+ 23.♕xd1 ♕e3** mate.

The attraction of the bishop sac becomes even more understandable when you look at the following game.

Klaus Klundt
Tigran Petrosian
Bamberg 1968
1.e4 c5 2.♘f3 e6 3.d4 cxd4 4.♘xd4 ♘f6 5.♘c3 d6 6.♗c4 a6 7.♗b3 b5 8.0-0 ♗b7

As soon as the c8-bishop has released the *überdeckung* of the e6-pawn, Whites lashes out with the bishop sac. The position is almost equal to the first game, with colours reversed (where, in fact, White (!) was a tempo down). The sacrifice probably came as a surprise for Petrosian, as it had not been played before in this position (although Euwe had mentioned it in the Zurich 1959 tournament book).
9.♗xe6!? fxe6 10.♘xe6 ♕d7 10...♕c8 seems the better square, leaving d7 for the b8-knight. This allows White to grab a third pawn for the piece with 11.♘xf8 ♖xf8 12.♕xd6, but then Black will develop easily and bring his king out of the danger zone, starting with 12...♔f7. The alternative is 11.♘d5 anyway, to keep the initiative going. **11.♘d5 ♗xd5 12.exd5** And the World Champion escaped with a draw by returning the piece: **12...♔f7 13.g4** 13.a4 (again with the idea of ♖a1-a3) or quick development with 13.♗g5 were good alternatives. **13...h6 14.f4 ♕a7+ 15.♔h1 ♘bd7 16.g5 ♕b7 17.gxf6 ♘xf6 18.♕f3 ♕xd5 19.f5 ♗e7 20.♗e3 g5 21.♖ad1 ♕xf3+ 22.♖xf3 ♖ac8 23.c3 ♘e8 24.♗d4 ♗f6 25.♖e3 ♗xd4 26.♖xd4 ♔f6 27.a4 ♖b8 28.♖b4 ½-½.**

Many bishop sacs on e6 have been seen in the Sicilian. However, if we focus on those resulting in a long-lasting initiative with a black king starting on e8, the true foundations were laid in... the Queen's Gambit Accepted! In this historic game.

José Raul Capablanca
Efim Bogoljubow
Moscow 1925
**1.d4 d5 2.c4 e6 3.♘f3 dxc4 4.e4 c5
5.♗xc4 cxd4 6.♘xd4 ♘f6 7.♘c3
♗c5 8.♗e3 ♘bd7**

9.♗xe6 'Capablanca felt morally obliged to play for a win in this game', wrote Bogoljubow, who also asserted he had provoked Capa's sac with his previous move. **9...fxe6 10.♘xe6 ♕a5?** Already the decisive mistake, since this leaves the octopus unchallenged. Although allowing an annoying pin, 10...♕b6 was necessary, when Capablanca suggested 11.♘xc5 ♘xc5 12.0-0, with the sample line 12...♕c6 13.♖c1 ♘cxe4 14.♘xe4 ♕xe4 15.♖e1 ♔f7 16.♖c7+ ♔g6 17.♗d4 ♕f4 18.♖ee7

18...♖d8 (in *My Great Predecessors* Kasparov noted at this point that 'even without a computer it is clear that after the simple 18...♖g8 there is no win for White. Still, after his suggested 19.♗e3 ♕b4 there is the quiet move 20.h3 (no more back-rank mate now) 20...♗f5 21.♕f3 when Black's rooks are just too passive and the black king is not going

'Capablanca felt morally obliged to play for a win in this game', wrote Bogoljubow.

to survive) 19.♖xg7+ ♔h6 20.♖xh7+!.
11.0-0! White simply develops, while Black will find it hard to do the same.
11...♗xe3 12.fxe3 Apart from ♘xg7+, White wants to continue with ♘c3-d5. **12...♔f7 13.♕b3 ♔g6 14.♖f5 ♕b6 15.♘f4+ ♔h6 16.g4?** Instead, 16.♕f7, threatening ♖h5, or ♕h5, and mate on the next move, would have earned Capablanca a trivial win after 16...g6 17.♘e6 ♕xe3+ 18.♔h1. **16...g5!** And after intricate complications Capa still prevailed, but in the end he could not prevent Bogoljubow from winning the tournament of his life: **17.♕xb6 axb6 18.♖d1! ♖g8 19.♘fd5 ♘xg4 20.♘e7 ♖g7 21.♖d6+ ♔h5 22.♖f3 ♘gf6 23.♖h3+ ♔g4 24.♖g3+ ♔h5 25.♘f5 ♖g6 26.♘e7 g4 27.♘xg6 ♔xg6 28.♖xg4+ ♔f7 29.♖f4 ♔g7 30.e5 ♘e8 31.♖e6 ♘c7 32.♖e7+** 1-0.

In the usually solid Caro-Kann things are slightly different, but no less complicated.

Mohammed Al-Modiahki
Evandro Barbosa
Incheon 2013
1.e4 c6 2.d4 d5 3.♘c3 dxe4 4.♘xe4 ♘d7 In the main line, Black's light-squared bishop is also deflected from the defence of the e6-pawn, although it is developed to an active position: 4...♗f5 5.♘g3 ♗g6 6.♘h3 (the well-known game Keres-Olafsson, Bled 1961, went 6.♗c4 e6 7.♘1e2 ♘f6 8.h4 h6 9.♘f4 ♗h7 10.♕e2 ♗d6 11.c3 – after 11.♗xe6, 11...0-0 is a typical way to refuse the sac, which you should keep in mind – 11...♘bd7 12.♗xe6 fxe6 – even here 12...0-0 is a sensible try – 13.♘xe6 ♕e7 14.♘f5) 6...♘f6 7.♘f4 ♘bd7 8.♗c4 ♕c7, a move that would usually

trigger the bishop sac even more. Still, the result is far from obvious here.
5.♘g5 ♘gf6 6.♗c4 e6 7.♘e2 h6 8.♘f3 ♗d6 9.♗f4 ♗xf4 10.♘xf4 ♕c7 11.♕d2 ♘b6 12.♗b3 c5 13.dxc5

13...♘bd7? 14.♗xe6 fxe6 15.♘xe6 ♕c6 16.♘fd4! ♕e4+ 17.♔f1

With the e-file open, things can get pretty hopeless for Black after the sacrifice, as Sicilian players have known at least since Averbakh-Taimanov, Zurich 1953.
17...♔f7 18.♖e1 ♕d5 Here the tactics work well for White, for instance 18...♕h4 19.♘c7 ♖b8 20.♖e7+. **19.♘c7 ♕xc5** Or 19...♕c4+ 20.♔g1 ♖b8 21.♘cb5 ♕xc5 22.b4 ♕h5 23.♘f5. **20.♘xa8 b6 21.♘e6 ♕c4+ 22.♔g1 ♗b7 23.♘ac7 ♖c8 24.♕d6 g5 25.h3 a6 26.♔h2 ♕xc2 27.♖hf1 g4 28.hxg4 ♘xg4+ 29.♔g1 ♘gf6 30.♖e3 ♖g8 31.♘d8+ ♖xd8 32.♕e7+ ♔g6 33.♕xd8 ♕c6 34.♖g3+ ♔f5 35.♘e8 ♘h5 36.♘g7+** 1-0.

Chess remains inexhaustible. Capa's sacrifice, while not immediately decisive, may certainly still teach us a thing or two about long-term initiatives! ∎

The Blitz Whisperer
Maxim Dlugy

The inimitable Karpov style... in blitz!

Perhaps he is not the first name that comes to mind for the younger generation, but Anatoly Karpov is one of the greatest blitz players of all time. **MAXIM DLUGY** was thrilled to have the former World Champion as a special guest during his Chess Max Academy summer camp in New York City. And of course some blitz was played...

The word 'Karpovian' is a familiar concept to anyone steeped in chess literature. But even less bookish aficionados will know its meaning: it's all about prophylactic thinking in chess, the purposeful pursuit of building small advantages, and the ability to maintain long-term pressure, while avoiding the slightest possibility of counterplay for your opponent.

Last year, in August, Anatoly Karpov graciously agreed to spend one full week at my Chess Max Academy in New York City, teaching a camp filled with talented children. One of the

highlights of the camp was that the students were paired up to play Karpov in a consultation blitz game. The time-control of 5 minutes with a 2 second delay allowed the youngsters some extra time for discussion between themselves. To my delight, the games were extremely well fought, especially on the top boards.

As I was watching the games, I was marvelling once again at how Anatoly uses his time and avoids counterplay, even at the price of finding a crushing *coup de grâce*. Still, he won every game without allowing any serious complications. Only in one game did he stand badly in the opening, but his unique

ability to unearth incredible defensive resources saved the day. His young opponents got so surprised that they simply forgot their main idea. This year Karpov will be back and I cannot wait to see more great chess moves from this great champion. Let me show you some of the ideas from last year's camp to give you an idea of why Anatoly Karpov was once the best blitz chess player in the world.

Anatoly Karpov
Christopher Yoo/Kim Yoon
New York, Karpov camp 2017
Grünfeld Indian, Exchange Variation

1.d4 ♘f6 2.c4 g6 3.♘c3 d5 4.cxd5 ♘xd5 5.e4 ♘xc3 6.bxc3 ♗g7 7.♘f3 c5 8.♕a4+

This sideline of the main line Grünfeld even caught Mr. Grünfeld, Peter Svidler, off-guard in the Russian Team Championship last year, when he barely made a draw from a losing position against Karpov. Christopher Yoo, currently the second-highest rated 11-year-old in the world, and Kim Yoon – currently rated 2360 in the FIDE list – are a formidable team together. After conferring they decided to play:

8...♘d7 9.♗e2 0-0 10.0-0 cxd4 11.cxd4 ♘b6 12.♕a3

12.♕b4 is also a reasonable attempt for a slight edge, but Karpov has his views.
12...♗g4 13.♗g5 ♗xf3 14.♕xf3
This somewhat unnatural move is a novelty, with both other captures having been tried in GM chess.

14...♕xd4
The young players don't like passive defence, and so stayed away from the more aggressive looking capture with the bishop on d4. After 14...♗xd4 15.♖ad1 ♕d6! 16.♔h1 e5 17.♕h3, planning f4, White has significant compensation for the pawn.
15.♗xe7 ♖fe8 16.♖ad1 ♕e5 17.♗d6 ♕xe4 18.♕xe4 ♖xe4 19.♗f3 ♖d4 20.♖xd4 ♗xd4 21.♖d1! Karpov rarely misses a useful in-between move. Here he improves the position of his rook 'for free' before capturing on b7.

Former World Champion Anatoly Karpov together with Christopher Yoo, the highest rated 11-year-old in the US, at this year's Chess Max Academy Karpov Camp.

21...♗f6 22.♗xb7 ♖d8 23.♗f3
White steers the game into a two bishops versus bishop and knight endgame. A long and gruelling defence awaits the youngsters.
23...♘a4!
The best reaction. The knight heads for c3, from where it will exert pressure on White's a-pawn.

24.♗b4 It's amazing that from this point on Karpov displays nearly perfect play, synching with Stockfish's top-three choices throughout.

24...♖b8 25.a3!
Though White's edge is minuscule, Black needs to play perfectly to neutralize it. For a while, the two talented masters are up to the task.
25...♘c3 26.♖e1 ♘b5! 27.♖d1 ♘d4 It seems Black forgot where they came from, or else 27...♘c3, forcing White to do something different, would have been logical.

28.♗e4 ♘e2+
It's very tempting to trade on c3, as it seems there is no danger in the opposite-coloured bishop endgame.
29.♔f1 ♘c3 30.♗xc3 ♗xc3 31.♖d7 a5 32.♗d5 ♖f8
The engines suggest immediately abandoning the pawn and playing the endgame a pawn down, but it's a difficult decision to make even in a tournament game.

'As I was watching the games, I was marvelling once again at how Anatoly uses his time and avoids counterplay.'

33.a4 ♗b4 34.f4

The pawns are of course placed on the colour of the opposing side's bishop – child's play for Anatoly!

34...♔g7 35.♔f2 h5 36.♔f3 ♔f6 37.g3 ♗e7 38.♖a7!

The bishop is forced to return to defending the pawn so that Black's rook doesn't get active.

38...♗b4

Of course, Black could always activate his rook, but after 38...♖c8 39.♖xa5 ♖c3+ 40.♔g2 ♖c2+ 41.♔h3 ♖c7 42.♗g2 ♔g7 43.♖a8, White would push the a-pawn up the board and the fight for the draw would continue.

39.h3 ♔g7 40.g4 hxg4+ 41.hxg4

41...♔f6?

With time running short, the idea 41...g5 42.fxg5 ♔g6, getting the king the much needed space in exchange for a pawn, needed to be played.

42.g5+ ♔g7 43.♔g4

I am always amazed at how great technicians are not afraid to go into drawish looking positions, as they know how to squeeze all the possible chances for a win in those games. It makes it much more difficult to face them when you are even only a little

> ## 'Great technicians are not afraid to go into drawish looking positions, as they know how to squeeze all the possible chances for a win.'

bit worse. Anatoly's threat is becoming clear: after breaking in with f5, he will be threatening to use the pin on the 7th rank with g6. Will Black have enough resources to survive then?

43...♗c3 44.f5

44...gxf5+?

After the game was over, we debated whether this was the decisive mistake. What happens if Black simply waits with, say, 44...♗b4 ? If White tries 45.f6+ ♔g8 46.♔f3 Black makes the king return with 46...♗d2. Though Black is ridiculously passive, I don't see a winning plan for White.

45.♔xf5 ♖e8? Seeing the threat

of g6, Black panics. The win was not obvious though, as after 45...♖e1 46.g6 ♗b4 47.gxf7 ♖h8, Black is planning the defensive manoeuvre ...♖h6-...f6 with good chances to save the game. Now it's all over.

46.♖xf7+ ♔h8 47.♖d7

One of the aspects of Karpov's style is to make sure all of your pieces are defended as much as possible.

47...♖f8+ 48.♔g6 ♗g7

The youngsters lay the last trap, in an attempt to stave off the mate on h7. Karpov smiles and... takes the bishop.

49.♖xg7 ♖f6+ 50.♔h5! ♖h6+ 51.♔g4!

The bishop is of course the 'right colour', so the trick simply fails.

51...♖d6 52.♖g8+ ♔h7 53.g6+ ♔h6 54.♗b3 ♖d3 55.♗c2 ♖d4+ 56.♔f3 ♖c4 57.♖h8+ ♔g7 58.♖h7+ Black resigned. I learned a lot from this simple-looking game.

In the next game, Karpov faces two young players rated about 1900 FIDE. They catch him in the opening and it seems an upset is in the making. Yet, Karpov starts displaying incredible creativity in finding resources to fight off seemingly unsolvable threats.

**Rushaan Maharaj/Henry Burton
Anatoly Karpov**
New York, Karpov camp 2017
Queen's Pawn Opening

1.d4 ♘f6 2.♗f4 d5 3.e3 c6 4.c4 ♗f5 5.♘c3 e6 6.♕b3

When I show the London System to my students, I call this 'Dream Position #2, with Dream Position #1 occurring after White's fourth move. The problem for Black is that the most natural move that Karpov plays here, lands him in a lot of trouble.

6...♛b6 7.c5! ♛xb3 8.axb3 ♞fd7
Karpov played this nearly instantly, clearly demonstrating that he is planning to play for ...e5 as soon as possible. **9.b4! f6 10.♞f3 g5 11.♗g3 h5 12.h3**

12...b6 This looks dangerous, but White's threat of 13.b5 forces some preventive reaction.
After 12...♚f7 13.♗e2 ♗e7 14.h4 g4 15.♞d2 e5 16.♞b3 White would also be better.
13.♗xb8 The young players grow impatient and try to win a pawn. It's not that easy. Building up the position with simple developing moves such as ♗e2 would be more 'Karpovian'.
13...♖xb8 14.b5!
An excellent move, not allowing Black play along the b-file.

14...♖c8?
This move, which Karpov played very quickly, defends the c6-square, but leaves the rest of the queenside unattended. It was best to bite the bullet and take on c5. After 14...bxc5 15.bxc6 ♞b6 16.♗b5 ♞d8 17.0-0 c4 18.♖xa7, Black has the excellent defensive resource 18...♖h7 with equality. Still, taking on a7 is not forced and White is significantly better after 18.e4 instead.
15.bxc6 ♞b8

16.cxb6?!
The first inaccuracy by the young team. After 16.♖xa7 ♞xc6 17.♖a6 bxc5 18.♗b5 ♚d7 19.dxc5 ♗xc5 20.♞a4 ♚d6 21.♚e2, Black would be helpless against the simple threat of ♖c1.
16...axb6 17.♖a8 ♚d8
Karpov is balancing on the brink here.
18.♗b5 ♖h7
The 7th rank is open and Black is trying to bring in pieces to help.

19.0-0?!
Another inaccuracy. After the aggressive 19.♞a4 ♞xc6 20.♖xc8+ ♚xc8 21.♗xc6 ♖c7 22.♞xb6+ ♚d8 23.♗a4 ♖c1+ 24.♚d1 ♗b4+ 25.♚e2 ♖b1 26.♞a4 ♗c2 27.♗xc2 ♖xh1 28.♞c5, White's objective advantage is decisive.

19...♖hc7

20.♖fa1? The final mistake that gives Black equality. After 20.♖c1 ♞xc6 21.♖xc8+ ♖xc8 22.♞xd5 exd5 23.♖xc6 ♖xc6 24.♗xc6, White would have an extra pawn with reasonable winning chances.
20...♞xc6 21.♗xc6?
The downward spiral continues. The bishops will clearly be stronger than the knights now.

21...♖xc6 22.♖xc8+ ♖xc8 23.♖a6 ♖b8 24.♞d2 ♗d3
And after valiantly fighting the former World Champion, the boys finally blundered with:

25.♖a3? ♗xa3 and resigned a few moves later.

I was impressed by how Karpov quickly moved all the pieces in the direction of his problematic queenside. Although against correct play it wouldn't have helped, the moves ...♘fd7, ...b6, ...♖c8, ...♔d8 and ...♖h7 were great to watch. Anatoly is ready to make as many moves as it takes to clear away all of his opponents' threats. This devotion to getting rid of his opponent's counterplay disoriented even the mighty Garry Kasparov, who in his first World Championship match against Karpov was having a very hard time guessing his rival's moves.

In the following game Karpov faces two players rated 2100 and 2200 in the U.S. During the game, Joseph continued to insist on the most aggressive moves possible, and for a while this approach kept the duo well in the game. But then Karpov unleashed his secret weapon...

And, of course, they wanted to see Anatoly Karpov play blitz against Maxim Dlugy, to

Anatoly Karpov
Joseph Zeltsan/Marcello Berger
New York, Karpov camp 2017
Nimzo-Indian, Classical Variation

1.d4 ♘f6 2.c4 e6 3.♘c3 ♗b4 4.♕c2 d5 5.a3 ♗xc3+ 6.♕xc3 0-0 7.♘f3 dxc4 8.♕xc4 b6 9.♗f4 ♗a6 10.♕a4

Here, 10.♕c2 and 10.♕xc7 were also tested in GM practice with Black managing a roughly 50% score.

10...♗b7 Black plays a very normal-looking move that happens to be a novelty. Instead, after 10...♕d7 11.♕xd7 ♘bxd7 12.e3 ♗xf1 13.♖xf1 c5 14.0-0-0 ♖ac8, Black should not have any opening problems.

11.♖c1 ♘bd7! An excellent intuitive sacrifice suggested by Joseph. Black could also weaken his queenside by playing ...c5, but this move may be stronger.

12.e3 Karpov senses the danger a mile away and avoids capturing the c-pawn. After 12.♗xc7 ♕e7 13.♗f4 ♗xf3 14.gxf3 ♖ac8 15.♖xc8 ♖xc8 16.♕xa7 e5 17.dxe5 ♘d5 18.♕b7 ♕c5 19.♗e3 ♘xe3 20.fxe3 ♘xe5, for example, it's clear Black is doing rather well.
12...c5 13.♗d6 ♖e8 14.dxc5 ♘xc5 15.♗xc5 bxc5
Karpov has established a superior pawn structure, but Black is quite active, as he has potential counterplay down the b-file. Some exact moves are required.

16.♗b5 ♖e7 17.0-0 ♕b6

18.♖c2 Anatoly begins his mission of over-protection. He plans to solidly defend all his pieces before beginning to attack. Another possibility was to play 18.♘e5.
18...♖d8?!
Black's move looks natural, but, as there are no entry squares on the d-file, misses the mark. It was important to play 18...♗e4 19.♖d2 ♖b8 20.♗e2 ♖eb7, lining up all the might on the b-file with a fine position.
19.♘d2 a6 20.♗e2 ♖ed7 21.♘c4 ♕c7 When I saw the next move, I immediately recognized the mark of Anatoly Karpov. White protects the bishop on e2 in anticipation of the rook entering d2 one day.

22.♖e1! After 22.♕a5 ♕xa5 23.♘xa5 ♖d2 24.♖xd2 ♖xd2 25.♖d1, White would have a nice advantage in the endgame, but simplification is not part of Karpov's plan.

Anatoly still had a minute and forty seconds on his clock, to his opponents' 2:45. But the moves come naturally now and the time disadvantage disappeared shortly. Setting up your position in blitz to make natural quick decisions is an essential element.

22...♘e4 23.♕a5! ♕b8 24.f3 ♘f6

25.♕xc5 With more time on the clock, I am sure Karpov would choose 25.e4, with full domination, but he decides to reap the reward of his labours instead. The youngsters seize their chance for counterplay.

25...♖d5 26.♕b4 ♖h5 27.g3

27...♘d5?

This move simply allows White to win time by pushing the knight back in a couple of moves. There was some play after 27...g5 28.f4 ♖b5 29.♕a4 ♗e4 30.♖d2 ♖bd5 31.♖ed1 h5 with chances to muddy the waters on the light squares.

28.♕b3 ♕a7 29.♖d2 ♖b8 30.♕d3

Karpov is positioning his pieces compactly to avoid blunders in time-pressure. There is no counterplay left.

30...f6 31.♕d4 ♕a8 32.e4 e5 33.♕f2 ♘e7 34.♖d7 ♘g6 35.♘d6 ♗c6 36.♗c4+ ♔h8 37.♖a7

Black resigned. The ability to produce moves such as 22.♖e1! in a blitz game separates Karpov from the mere mortals. After the game I asked his opponents if they understood the point of 22.♖e1. Both of them shook their heads.

In the final game that we look at, Karpov wins with his incredible technique. It's a perfect example of why endgame specialists are especially strong in blitz.

Daniel Johnston/Sumit Dhar
Anatoly Karpov
New York, Karpov camp 2017
Caro-Kann, Two Knights Variation

1.e4 c6 2.♘f3 d5 3.♘c3 ♗g4 4.h3 ♗xf3 5.♕xf3 e6 6.d4 ♘f6 7.♗g5 ♗e7 8.0-0-0 dxe4 9.♘xe4 ♘xe4 10.♗xe7 ♕xe7 11.♕xe4 ♘d7 12.c4

With over 20 games in the database, this move had not been played once. Karpov takes over a minute here to decide on his reply. To the naked eye the difference between 12...♘f6 and 12...0-0 is not worth such a time investment, but for Karpov this was an important moment. I would love to be strong enough to understand his thinking here.

12...♘f6

On 12...0-0 play could continue 13.g4 ♘f6 14.♕e3.

13.♕e3 0-0

14.♗d3?!

This is a serious inaccuracy. White needs to be fast in building up pressure on the kingside, and the bishop may be needed elsewhere. After the correct 14.g4, I like White's prospects a little more.

14...罝ad8 The opportunity for excellent positional counterplay with 14...b5! was available for Black. White is simply worse after this move.

15.含b1 Once again 15.g4 was stronger here.

15...罝d6 16.总c2 罝fd8 17.罝d2 豐d7 18.罝hd1 c5

Black's methodical build-up doesn't guarantee him an advantage. White's bishop gives the young consultation team good counterchances.

19.d5! exd5 20.豐xc5 b6 21.豐a3 d4 22.g4 豐c7 23.豐d3 g6 24.罝e1 a5 25.总d1

The understanding of how to improve one's position is extremely important in blitz play. Karpov gradually crawls his pieces into better spots, while White is struggling for ideas. It was best to give the king some air with 25.a3.

25...罝c6 26.罝c2?

It was very difficult to see that White should welcome Black's capture on c4, as the bishop would be quite strong on b3 in that case. Instead of this passive defence, White should have played 26.罝de2 罝xc4 27.总b3 罝c5 28.豐d2!, aiming at Black's king, with excellent counterplay for the pawn.

26...罝c5 A hidden opportunity that would secure Black's advantage was 26...包d7 27.豐xd4 包c5 28.豐c3 罝e6!!, winning material. A nice combination for the books.

27.总f3 豐f4 28.罝e7 罝dc8 Here, 28...包d7 was stronger, but White's defensive task is getting tougher by the move.

29.罝b7

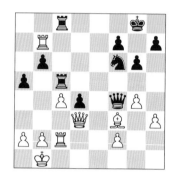

It's natural to look for a counterattack, although 29.a4 would have been more sound, giving the king an exit and blocking Black's ...b5 forever.

29...含g7!

Karpov played this instantly, setting up a trap. The pawn is poisoned, and White would do best to play a waiting move such as 30.a3.

30.罝xb6?! 包d7! 31.罝b3 a4 32.罝a3 包e5 33.豐e4 豐xe4 34.总xe4 包xc4

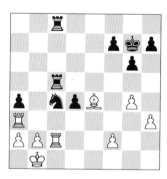

The threat of 35...包d2+ forces White's rook to remain on the third rank.

35.罝d3 f5! 36.gxf5 gxf5 Anatoly played this whole sequence extremely rapidly, clearly expecting that White has to lose material. Indeed, if White's bishop moves off the b1-h7 diagonal, Black will win material with ...包a3+.

37.罝g3+

37...含f6?!

This natural king move is an inaccuracy. Best was 37...含h6 38.总d3 包d2+ 39.含c1 包f1 – the point is that after 40.罝g1 罝xc2+ 41.含xc2 d3 42.罝xf1 罝xc2+ 43.含b1 f4 Black has a winning rook and pawn endgame.

38.总d3 包d2+ 39.含c1 包e4

40.总xe4 After 40.罝f3 含e5 41.h4 罝5c6 42.罝xc6 罝xc6+ 43.总c2 罝c8, Black would be much better as well.

40...fxe4 41.罝xc5 罝xc5+ 42.含d2?

Helping the rook get to c2 with check is a mistake. After 42.含d1! 罝f5 43.含e2 罝b5 44.b3 h5 45.含d2 axb3 46.罝xb3 罝xb3 47.axb3 含e5 48.含e2 h4 49.f3 e3 50.b4 含f4 51.b5 d3+ 52.含xd3 含xf3 53.b6 e2 54.b7 e1豐 55.b8豐 the position is a tablebase draw.

42...♖g5!? Karpov quickly assesses the king and pawn endgame as winning for him. The direct 42...d3! was immediately decisive as after 43.♔d1 ♖c2 44.♖e3 ♔f5 45.f3 exf3 46.♖xf3+ ♔e4 47.♖f7 ♖xb2 48.♖xh7 ♖xa2 49.♖e7+ ♔d4 50.♖d7+ ♔c3 51.♖c7+ ♔b3 52.♖b7+ ♔a3 53.♖d7 ♖h2 54.♖xd3+ ♔b2, White is helpless against the advance of the a-pawn.

43.♖a3?

The proof of the pudding is in the eating. The talented duo could have noticed that the outside b-pawn and the possibility of breaking up Black's pawn structure with f3 at the right moment afforded them drawing chances. Biting the bullet with 43.♖xg5! ♔xg5 44.b3 axb3 45.axb3 ♔f4 46.b4 ♔f3 47.♔e1 d3 48.b5 d2+ 49.♔xd2 ♔xf2 50.b6 e3+ 51.♔d3 e2 52.b7 e1♕ 53.b8♕ would have secured a draw.

43...♖b5 44.♔c2 In time pressure, White touched the king and produced this mistake. After the best 44.b3 axb3 45.axb3 ♔e5 46.♖a7 h5 47.h4 ♖xb3 48.♖a5+ ♔f4 49.♖xh5 ♖b2+ 50.♔e1 d3 51.♖h8 ♖e2+ 52.♔f1 White should hold the game.

44...♖b4?

In mutual time-pressure Karpov misses 44...♖f5, winning the f2-pawn and the game.

45.b3 axb3+ 46.axb3 ♖b7 47.♖a4 ♔e5 48.♖a5+?

The final mistake in this hard-fought game. White's rook had to look for activity: 48.♖a8 ♖f7 49.♖e8+ ♔f4 50.♔d2 ♔f3 51.♖e5 and White miraculously holds this dangerous position.

48...♔f4 49.♖a6 d3+ 50.♔c3 ♖c7+ 51.♔d2 ♖c2+

52.♔d1

A mistake, but after the best move 52.♔e1, Black could win instructively with 52...♖e2+ 53.♔f1 ♔e5 54.♖a7 ♔d4 55.♖xh7 ♔c3 56.♖a7 ♖c2 57.♖c7+ ♔b2 58.♖d7 ♔c1 59.h4 d2.

52...♖xf2 53.b4 ♖b2 54.♖b6 e3 55.♖f6+ ♔e5 56.♖f3 ♖b1 Mate.

As we can see from these examples, even today, almost 20 years after he retired from active tournament play, Anatoly Karpov's resolute style makes him a formidable blitz player. I would point out the following traits that account for his continued prowess:

1 He keeps everything protected. Karpov knows the benefits of 'over-protecting' his pieces. Overprotected pieces don't need permission to start attacking, as their colleagues will remain defending the base.

2 Cool defence. Many players, when attacked in blitz, prefer to panic. Karpov instead looks for new pieces that can help in the defence. The ability to find many defensive moves in a row can exasperate most aggressive opponents.

3 Step-by-step position improvement. Karpov is never in a hurry. He painstakingly looks for ways to improve his position in the most subtle ways before he strikes. Even though it makes him miss some winning shots, it also ensures an incredibly stable performance over the long haul.

4 Excellent endgame technique. It's very difficult to play someone who will always try to convert the smallest advantage. ∎

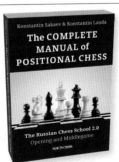

Something for everyone

Quiet openings, wild openings, tough middlegames and wonderful endgames, **MATTHEW SADLER** reviews a rich and varied bouquet of new chess books.

T he summer months have been busy for me because I combine working from home with frequent train trips abroad as my French-Belgian-Dutch projects pick up pace. Undoubtedly due to my staggeringly great importance, I have been provided with an extremely large work laptop, which is too wide and deep to be able to work comfortably in a standard seat! After half an hour of unsociably elbowing my neighbour, it's time to put the computer away and reach for a chess book and a pocket set. A perfect opportunity to catch up with some book reviewing... Unfortunately, there's something about a pocket chess set that fascinates people and I have spent many trips chatting about chess with my neighbour rather than reading books. I'm finally discovering chess as a way of making friends!

We start off with *How Ulf beats Black* (New In Chess) by the prolific American author Cyrus Lakdawala. This 287-page book provides a complete repertoire for White based around the 'bulletproof' openings Ulf Andersson used in his heyday in the 70s and 80s. The author – whose own opening repertoire is based on Ulf's lines – describes discovering Ulf's games in the early 1980's to seeing 'a cosmic vision' and he 'pursued a lifelong quest to discover its inner meaning.' He describes Ulf's repertoire and style as operating 'in a kind parasitic fashion, sucking the vitality out of the game, where only strategic considerations and endgame skills count.'

The book presents 61 complete games of which 15 are by the author himself. There are also 39 exercises based on positions from Ulf's games. The opening comments are fairly detailed but – appropriately for a repertoire based around typical positions rather than rote learning – the resulting middlegames and endgames get the most attention. I'll give you a sample of the treats in store for you. Against the King's Indian, Lakdawala recommends the Exchange Variation, of course:

Exchange King's Indian
1.♘f3 ♘f6 2.c4 g6 3.♘c3 ♗g7 4.e4 d6 5.d4 0-0 6.♗e2 e5 7.dxe5 dxe5 8.♕xd8 ♖xd8 9.♗g5

Against the Grünfeld, we get this line:

Anti-Grünfeld
1.♘f3 ♘f6 2.c4 g6 3.♘c3 d5 4.cxd5 ♘xd5 5.e4 ♘xc3 6.dxc3 ♕xd1+ 7.♔xd1

This type of repertoire is not everyone's cup of tea, but any player would benefit from being able to play in this fashion from time to time. I enjoyed the book in general. The games are excellent, including many of Ulf's famous queenless middlegames, and Lakdawala is a chatty and engaging writer, although readers may not always connect with his analogies. A comment like 'The way I looked at a piece grab 18.♗xb6!? was: it's similar to the greedy man who murders his 105-year-old aunt to inherit her money. It's a bad gamble. If he waits it out for a few months, or, at the most, a year, it allows nature to do its dirty work on her decaying body, and he gets the money without risk of imprisonment of life' is evocative, but perhaps overdoing it somewhat.

From the chess point of view, there were two things that disturbed me. Firstly, the exact move orders to follow as White were not completely clear to me. For example, 1.♘f3 is the obvious start, but after 1...d5, I wasn't at all sure what Lakdawala was recommending. There is a chapter on 1.♘f3 d5 2.c4 and this is the move order given in the index of variations at the end of the book, but Lakdawala's comments are not enthusiastic: 'Today, I believe that White gets better chances not allowing Black to play 2...d4 by playing 2.d4 or 2.g3' and after 2...d4: 'Ulf hasn't scored well against this move'. However, playing 2.d4 or 2.g3 would lead to a swathe of opening lines not covered in the book.

Secondly, some of the lines Ulf plays have been completely (I'd almost say mathematically) neutralised. Take the Exchange King's Indian:

Exchange King's Indian
1.♘f3 ♘f6 2.c4 g6 3.♘c3 ♗g7 4.e4 d6 5.d4 0-0 6.♗e2 e5 7.dxe5 dxe5 8.♕xd8 ♖xd8 9.♗g5 ♖e8 10.♘d5 ♘xd5 11.cxd5 c6 12.♗c4 cxd5 13.♗xd5 ♘d7 14.♘d2 ♘c5 15.0-0-0 ♗e6 16.♗xe6 ♘xe6

Lakdawala quotes one of his own games which ended here in a draw with the comment 'I would normally decline the draw offer and play on if my opponent were a non-GM', which read to me as an original way of not saying anything about the position. In fact, as Bologan demonstrates in his recent book on the King's Indian, Black has no problems after:

17.♗e3 ♘f4

In fact, it's also easy for White to get worse if he's not careful. This doesn't invalidate the repertoire – the risk of absolute equality is inherent to the Ulf repertoire – but I didn't feel there was a need to ignore such possibili-

How Ulf beats Black
by Cyrus Lakdawala
New In Chess, 2018
★★★☆☆

ties when they arise, especially when they are well-known (I believe Joe Gallagher recommended this line for Black already in a King's Indian book published around 2000). Not perfect, but some interesting stuff there and some great Ulfie games!

■ ■ ■

Chess lessons (Russell Enterprises) is the much-missed legendary Russian coach Mark Dvoretsky's penultimate

Chess Lessons
by Mark Dvoretsky
Russell Enterprises, 2018
★★★★★

of chess openings, this book is laden with discoveries that both amaze and inspire.

Dvoretsky explains in his foreword that he always liked to start with games or fragments that had been analysed by annotators he respected. This gave him a first cursory impression of whether some useful information could be drawn from this example. If the example withstood intensive examination, Dvoretsky added it to those used

'This type of repertoire is not everyone's cup of tea, but any player would benefit from being able to play in this fashion from time to time.'

work and it's a very good one. In some of his recent works – I'm thinking of the recent *Maneuvering – The Art of Piece Play* (Russell Enterprises) – the puzzle element became too predominant in my view. I like solving difficult exercises from time to time, but I like reading what Mark has to say about a position even more. The fragmented puzzle format interfered with that pleasure!

This book strikes a balance that works better for me: there are many exercises throughout the text, but thanks to the book layout, the reader can choose whether to exercise his grey matter or just continue enjoying the analysis that Dvoretsky has brought together. And there is plenty to enjoy, not least the astounding breadth of material. Historic and modern games, famous and little-known brilliancies, covering the entire gamut

in his training work with students and this inevitably led to fresh discoveries as the brightest minds in Russian chess attempted to solve the problems set before them. In recent times, computer analysis added fresh insights. The material in the book has thus ripened over 30 years of study.

The remarkable thing about working with Dvoretsky as a coach was that his ability to find mistakes in your analysis was matched by his sincerity in wanting you to improve as a player. His evident and unabated enthusiasm to discover new truths in chess positions always managed to soften the blow to my ego of seeing the flaws revealed in my play and my understanding! This same quality makes the book such an enjoyable read.

Take this example: I was both distraught that one of my favourite manoeuvres turned out to be a mistake, and full of admiration for Dvoretsky's ingenuity in unravelling the position.

Lembit Oll
Julian Hodgson
Groningen 1993

position after 34.♗d6

In this position, Julian played an astonishing idea to activate his rook on d8, and it's an idea that has stuck in my mind forever!
34...♔h7 35.♕c5 ♔g6 36.h4 ♖h8 37.a3 ♖h5

'The material in the book has thus ripened over 30 years of study.'

How good is that? The black rook is coming into play via f5!
38.♕g1 ♔h7 39.♖d1 ♕b3 40.♖d2 ♖f5 41.g4 ♖f4 42.♕b1+ ♔g8 43.g5 b4 44.♖d3 ♘c3 45.axb4 ♕a2+ 46.♕xa2 ♖f1+ 0-1.
However, let's go back to the position after 34...♔h7.

While acknowledging Julian's creativity, Dvoretsky refuses to get carried away by the emotional power of this idea (as I have done for the past 25 years!) and finds some interesting defences for White.
35.a4 is a suggestion from Motylev, which allows White to fight for the 4th rank with his major pieces and seems to offer the best drawing chances. 35.♕c2 ♕xc2 36.♖xc2 f5 37.♖c5 is another idea Dvoretsky puts forward, when the ending after 37...g5 38.♖xb5 f4 is not clearly a win for Black.

35...bxa4 36.♕c4 Threatening 37.♕h4+ picking up the rook on d8!
36...♕xc4 37.♖xc4 f5 38.♖h4+ ♔g8 39.♖xa4 g5 40.♖xa5

Again this looks a long way from a Black win.

Finally, Dvoretsky tries to find the decisive advantage he feels is in the initial position (see first diagram on p.88):
34...b4

This is Dvoretsky's favourite idea, clamping down on White's queenside and restricting the white king, which improves any resulting endgames. This line was one that appealed to me. 34...g5 is another great idea, aiming to implement Julian's idea via ...♔g7, ...g4 and ...♖h8(-h5-f5)!

35.♕c2 ♕xc2 36.♖xc2 f5 37.h4 ♘f6 38.♖c5 ♘e4 39.♖xa5 ♘xg3 40.♖b5 ♘e4 41.♖xb4 ♘xd6 42.exd6

and now a precise sequence typical of Dvoretsky's analysis:
42...e5 43.♖b5 f4 44.♖xe5 f3 45.♖e1 f2 46.♖f1 ♖e8

Who would have guessed you could ignore White's passed d6-pawn to win the game?

All said, a fascinating book.

■ ■ ■

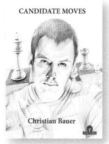

Candidate Moves by Christian Bauer Thinkers Publishing, 2018
★★★★☆

The next book on my reading list was *Candidate Moves* by Christian Bauer (Thinkers Publishing). I'm a big fan of the French GM, who reminds me a lot of the late, great Tony Miles in his attitude and style. He plays a huge number of games every year, and just like Tony he is not afraid of exploring the murkier side of chess theory, backing up this creativity with great fighting spirit and courage. A player who meets Ivan Sokolov's 1.d4 with 1...a6 in a crucial board 1 encounter and nearly wins (as I saw him do at

White's perspective and then from Black's.... Looking at a game from White's standpoint and then from Black's aims, in my view, at diminishing the subjective portion of the analysis, even though one will often naturally feel more sympathy for one camp or the other in a given position.' It sounded interesting, but I hadn't expected each game to be annotated twice: once from the White point of view and once from Black's. It also took me a long time to cotton on to how the annotations differed from each other. In fact, in the games from the White point of view only the White moves are annotated, and vice versa. I think it was worth mentioning this clearly in the preface, because it doesn't jump out at you from a first read of the book. While I'm busy expressing slight confusion,

'It sounded interesting, but I hadn't expected each game to be annotated twice: once from the White point of view and once from Black's.'

the Maastricht tournament in 2017) is worth appreciating in the percentages world of professional chess!

This book is a collection of 41 games by Christian played between 2007 and 2017, mostly wins with a few draws and losses thrown in. There are tough games against world-class players such as Nepomniachtchi, Bacrot and Leko, interesting wins against 2200s and many games against players of Bauer's own strength. I was excited when I received the book and was looking forward to playing through the games.

There is however something odd about the book, and even having read the preface, I wasn't prepared for the execution. Bauer explains that 'I found the idea to switch sides. By this I mean to look at games from

I will also mention that the title and the blurb 'Christian tackles one of the most important issues in chess: how to select candidate moves' didn't ring a bell with me. It wasn't something that I noticed as a driving theme throughout the book.

All those little gripes aside, I still enjoyed the book! The games are full of incident and there is lots of opening insight throughout the book. Bauer frequently describes a seemingly unrelated opening line that provided inspiration for an idea in the current game. Bauer's play is also extremely attractive: playing consistently for the win, he has a knack for injecting tension into positions, which makes the games both fun to play through and worthy of further study. The jury's still out on Bauer's innovation of annotating games from each side individually, as I often found myself flicking back and forth to try and get a coherent complete picture of the game. For me the book was a good effort, somewhere between 3 and 4 stars, but bathing in the sun on the tropical island of England, I feel generous today! 4 stars!

■ ■ ■

From the chaos of the International Open circuit to the serenity of stratospheric-level chess with Tibor Karolyi's 267-page exploration of Magnus Carlsen's endgame play: *Endgame Virtuoso Magnus Carlsen* (New In Chess). Karolyi uses a format similar to his recent 3-volume biography of Tal for Quality Chess. He presents the endings in chronological order, providing a summary per year of Magnus' tournament results, age, FIDE rating and world ranking. We follow Magnus' endgame play through his early years all the way through to his reign as World Champion. Karolyi typically enters the game at the start of the ending or just before the transition to the endgame. This book comprises 91 such game fragments played between 1999 (when Magnus was just 9 years old!) and 2017.

The annotations are generally light – about a sentence per annotated move – with occasionally some much deeper analysis at complicated or critical positions. I enjoyed the book: it's a perfect level to read in the train without a board, or to spend half an hour at home relaxing behind a board, marvelling at Carlsen's astonishing ingenuity in finding new ways to tie up his opponents with only minimal material on the board. It would be a good book to inculcate juniors into the joy of playing endgames! Recommended!

■ ■ ■

And finally, I got around to taking a serious look at Ivan Sokolov's second volume of *Chess Middlegame Strategies* for Thinkers Publishing called *Opening Meets Middlegame*. As Ivan

Endgame Virtuoso Magnus Carlsen by Tibor Karolyi New In Chess, 2018
★★★★☆

Chess Middlegame Strategies Volume 2 by Ivan Sokolov Thinkers Publishing, 2018
★★★★☆

explains in the Preface, he originally conceived the book as treating pure middlegame material but the focus moved more to the transition from certain openings to typical middlegames. Ivan covers a range of typical scenarios arising from 5 openings: the Sicilian, the Ruy Lopez, the 4...♘f6 Caro-Kann, the Benoni and the Catalan, finishing with an intriguing little chapter detailing a spot on the sun of Anatoly's Karpov positional judgement: a love of bishops that sometimes clouds his appreciation of the power of an opponent's knight. I'm not quite sure how that fits in with the rest of the chapters, but I'll never complain about interesting free extra chapters!

The themes covered are spectacular. We see 4 piece sacrifices: Velimirovic's amazing ♘(x)e6 in the Sicilian, knight sacrifices against e4 and d5 in the Classical Ruy Lopez (including a great game Polgar-Sokolov), Salem's and Kasparov's ...♘g4 in the Benoni and ♘xf7 in the Catalan. We've also got Petrosian's famous exchange sacrifice (allowing a rook on f1 to be taken by Black's light-squared bishop) against the Modern Benoni as well as a host of more positional themes in the Sicilian. You can see Ivan's work as a coach paying off here as a number of these openings are not ones I would associate with him!

Ivan's analysis can get quite dense at times, but despite that he does a good job of never losing his readers by taking time for summaries and explanations and by daring to formulate general rules. Take this extract from the introduction to the Sicilian theme: the fortified knight on e5.

Fortified knight on e5

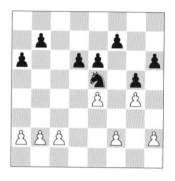

'Black has arguably weakened his kingside by the ...g7-g5-pawn push but on the other hand, he has safeguarded the dominant position of his knight on e5 by preventing White from expelling it with f2-f4. Black tries to maintain his strong knight's position on e5, pushes ...b7-b5 and gets queenside play as White always castles queenside in these lines. Black castles queenside or keeps his king in the centre, depending on the situation. Keeping his king in the centre is a risky strategy for Black. White often has a knight sacrifice on f5, opening the e-file after Black takes with ...exf5 and getting a direct attack on the Black king.'

Sokolov then goes on to give White 5 'rules' for storming the Black position. As a Sicilian Najdorf player for all of my professional career, I have played these structures a lot but I had not consciously understood them as clearly as Sokolov explains them. It's knowledge that is normally only gleaned when you discuss an opening with an expert, so it's wonderful to read this in a book!

All in all, an excellent work, in complexity probably best suited to a level of player a little higher than for Ivan's previous volume (2100+). Recommended! ■

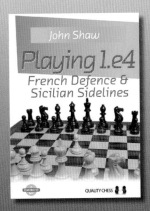

Judit Polgar

The beauty of getting better

Studies are aesthetically pleasing and intellectually challenging, but they also help you become a better player, as **JUDIT POLGAR** compellingly shows.

From when I was a kid, solving studies always was an important part of my daily training. At different stages in my career, my father, with his huge book collection, my early trainer Tibor Florian and former world title Candidate Pal Benko, helped and stimulated me in this direction. My favourite study composer is Leonid Kubbel, whose starting positions are very natural, as if taken from practical games. But I also like Richard Réti's studies, for their technical and theoretical character.

Studies are not only enjoyable for their beauty and creativity; they are also very useful if you want to improve your endgame technique and calculating abilities. As an active study solver, it often happened that at a crucial moment in an endgame I would suddenly remember a thematic manoeuvre from a study that

I had solved at some point in the past. Here is such a game, which I won at the age of 11.

Sigurdur Sigfusson
Judit Polgar
Reykjavik 1988

position after 52.♔xg4

In the inevitable pawn race, Black (to move) will be a tempo up, but only in

certain circumstances will this ensure a clear win in the ensuing queen ending. Fortunately, I was familiar with the idea of keeping the enemy king away from my pawn from a study composed by Grigoriev (see below).

52...♔e4! 53.♔h3 ♔f3 54.g4 ♔f4! The start of a mechanism aimed at forcing the enemy king to the exposed h5-square.

55.♔h4 d5 56.g5 ♔f5 57.♔h5 d4 58.g6 d3 59.g7 d2 60.g8♕

60...d1♕+ Gaining an essential tempo and soon transposing to another, this time trivially won, pawn ending.

61.♔h6 ♕h1+ 62.♔g7 ♕g2+

> 'It often happened that at a crucial moment I suddenly remembered a thematic manoeuvre from a study I had solved.'

63.♔f8 ♕xg8+ 64.♔xg8 ♔e6 65.♔f8 ♔d5 66.♔e7 ♔c4 0-1.

One of the studies that inspired me during this game was the following one:

N. Grigoriev
White to play and win
Izvestia 1928

1.♔d4! The same kind of prophylactic play as in my game. The hurried 1.f4 leads to a draw after 1...♔b5.

1...b5 Black is not in time to bring his king closer to the enemy pawn: 1...♔b5 2.♔d5 ♔a6 3.f4 ♔b7 4.f5 ♔c7 5.♔e6 ♔d8 6.♔f7 (shouldering the black king) 6...b5 7.f6 b4 8.♔g7 b3 9.f7 b2 10.f8♕+.

2.f4 b4 3.f5 b3

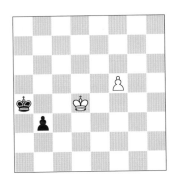

4.♔c3! Forcing the enemy king to advance to a3, similar to my play in the second phase of the game in the Reykjavik Open.

4...♔a3 5.f6 b2 6.f7 b1♕ 7.f8♕+
This time it is not about exchanging queens but about mating or winning the enemy queen. 1-0.

Sometimes it happened the other way around: after playing an interesting endgame I would sometimes compose a closely related study myself:

**Alexey Shirov
Judit Polgar**
Dortmund 1996

position after 50.♔d5

Objectively speaking, White has only vague winning chances, but it could be unpleasant for me to defend this position for a long time. So after Shirov's natural

51.♔b4?!
I immediately started checking for a way to reach a forced draw. Before simplifying to a pawn ending, one needs to calculate very accurately, since there is no place for assessments like ± or ±. The current position is either drawn or lost.

51...♗xd3! Shirov probably did not consider this move seriously, because his king is so close to my queenside pawns, and retrieving the pawn will cost me a couple of tempi.

52.cxd3 ♔d4 53.♔a5 ♔xd3 54.♔b6 ♔c2

55.a4 After 55.♔xb7 the only saving move is 55...a5 56.a4 (or, if 56.♔b6, then 56...a4 57.♔a5 ♔xb2) 56...♔b3!, followed by 57...♔xa4.

55...♔b3 Actually, I had an alternative: 55...a5 56.♔xa5 ♔b3 57.♔b5 b6,

leading to mutual zugzwang, exactly as in the game!

But I had calculated the game continuation until the end, using an idea that had been familiar to me since the age of 10.

56.a5

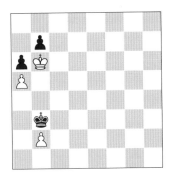

56...♔a4! The point! Black needs a small triangulation in order to put White in zugzwang. After 56...♔b4? 57.b3! the zugzwang would be... mine! Now, in view of the obvious line 57.b3+ ♔b4, reaching the same position as above but with White to move, we agreed to a draw.

The intriguing kings' dialogue in the presence of this particular queenside structure inspired me to compose the following study:

J. Polgar
White to play and win
Chess Life & Review 1997

1.♔g7 ♔g2 2.♔f6 ♔f3 3.♔e5!
Shouldering the enemy king. **3...♔e3** Black has no time for 3...a5 due to 4.♔d6, followed by ♔c7. **4.a5!!** This move will be necessary, anyway, in order to prevent ...b5 after ♔c7. And for the time being, e5 is the best square for the white king.

4.♔d6? would free the enemy king: 4...♔d3 5.a5 ♔c4 6.c7 ♔b5.

4.♔d5? may look like an improvement, but is actually a waste of time, since the king will not really approach the b7-pawn: 4...a5! 5.♔c5 ♔d3 6.♔b6 ♔c2 7.♔xb7 ♔b3!, with a familiar position from the previous game.

4...♔d3 5.♔d5

More shouldering.

5...♔c2

White has to decide how to attack the b7-pawn.

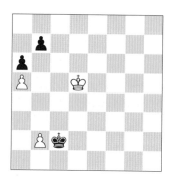

6.♔d6!!

Preparing to put Black in zugzwang. The natural move is 6.♔c5?, keeping the king closer to the action: 6...♔b3!! 7.♔b6 ♔a4! 8.b3+ ♔b4, with the same mutual zugzwang position that saved me against Shirov.

6...♔b3 7.♔c5!

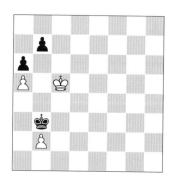

Triangulating and shouldering at the same time!

7...♔a4 8.♔b6 ♔b4 9.b3!

In contrast to my game, here it was Black who ended up in zugzwang. 1-0.

And here's one more 'practical' example. White would not have missed a win in

the next famous game if he had remembered (or known) a study pattern.

**Peter Svidler
Vishy Anand**
Dos Hermanas 1999

position after 69.h6

I was standing close to the board and was proud to have seen the winning line for White, but much to my surprise, the players agreed a draw after **69...♔f7**

It is obvious that the only winning attempt **70.♔xd4** allows **70...♘b5+ 71.♔c5 ♘xa7**

But the game would not end here: **72.♔b6!**

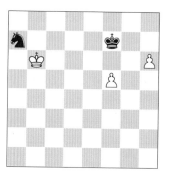

72...♘c8+

72...♔g8 73.f6! indirectly defends both pawns, and if 73...♘c8+ then 74.♔c7 ♘a7 75.♔d7+−.

73.♔c7 ♘e7

73...♘a7 74.♔d7 promotes the f-pawn by force, with two possible echo-variations in which the white king either goes to e7 or e8, depending on the knight's position: 74...♘b5 (or if 74...♔f6 then 75.h7 ♔g7 76.f6+ ♔xh7 77.f7 ♔g7 78.♔e8!+−) 75.h7 ♔g7 76.f6+ ♔xh7 77.f7 ♔g7 78.♔e7+−.

74.h7 ♔g7 74...♘d5+ 75.♔d6 does not change much.

75.f6+! The point. White queens one of the pawns.

This final trick has been used by composers more than once, but here is a study featuring the final part of the previous analysis with switched wings but everything else almost identical:

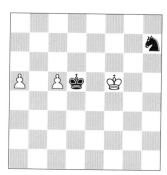

K. Stoichev
White to play and win
Shakhmatna Misl 1997

1.a6 ♔c6 The only difference is that the king is on c6 instead of on c7 (f7 without the wing switch).

2.♔g6 ♘f8+ 3.♔f7 ♘h7 3...♘d7 4.a7 ♔b7 5.c6+ leads to a perfect transposition to the above line. **4.♔e7 ♘g5 5.a7 ♔b7 6.c6+ ♔xa7 7.c7 ♔b7 8.♔d7** And again we are in a familiar situation.

Conclusion

■ Although studies are created 'artificially', solving them increases one's endgame understanding, imagination and calculating skills.

■ Even in seemingly simple positions, one should search for resources and try to calculate to the logical end. ■

1. Mareco-De Dovitiis
Montevideo 2018

34...♖d1+ Now 35.♗xd1 ♕xd1+ 36.♔g2 ♕e2+ is mate. After **35.♔g2 ♖g1+!** forced resignation due to 36.♔xg1 ♗h2+, winning the queen.

2. Dzhumaev-Iljiushenok
Voronezh 2018

Black can protect his knight with the c-pawn! **49...♖g1+ 50.♔h4 ♖g5!** White resigned on account of 51.♔xg5 c1♕+ followed by 52...♕xa3.

3. Krejci-Plat
Prague 2018

36.♖xd5 cxd5 37.♖e8! ♖xe8 38.dxe8♕+ ♔xe8 39.♗xf8 ♔xf8 40.♔g2 ♔e7 41.f4! Creating a remote passed pawn. Black resigned.

4. Adair-Sarakauskas
England tt 2018

38.g4! hxg4 Now the king is shielded by the enemy pawn. **39.♖f7 ♖2f4** 39...♔g6 loses to 40.♖xf5 ♖xf5 41.♔xg4. **40.♗xf5+ ♔g8 41.♔g5!** ♖xc4 42.♔g6 And Black resigned shortly after.

5. Kravtsiv-Rozum
Bhubaneswar 2018

25.♘d8! ♖xe2 25...♔g7 26.♘xe6+ ♔h6 27.g5 mate; 25...♔e8 26.♘xf7 ♗xf7 27.♗b5+; 25...♘e7 26.♘xe6+ ♔g8 27.♘d4 ♔f8 28.e6 leads to heavy losses. **26.♘xe6+ ♔e8** And Black resigned in view of 27.♖a4!.

6. Flores-Shankland
Montevideo 2018

The direct 26.♘f6+! would have won: 26...gxf6 27.♕g4+ ♔h8 28.♕f5! ♗xf2+ (28...♘e6 29.♗b1 ♘g5 30.♕xf6+ and wins) 29.♔xf2 ♖xc3 30.♕xf6+ and 31.♕xc3; 26...♔h8 27.♕d3 g6 28.♗xf7! and 29.♕xg6.

7. Lomasov-Sviridov
Yaroslavl 2018

White lost after the feeble **32.h3?**, missing the vigorous 32.♘e5! ♖xf2 (32...♘e2+ 33.♕xe2 dxe5 34.♕xh5) 33.♘g6+! ♔xh7 34.♘f8+ ♔g8 35.♕h7+! ♔xf8 36.♖xf2+ ♗f6 37.♖xf6+ exf6 38.♕xd7 and wins.

8. Rozentalis-Bernotas
Palanga 2018

38.♘h5+! ♔g6 38...♘xh5 39.♖h6+; 38...♔g5 39.♖e5+ ♔xg4 40.f3+! ♔xf3 41.♖f7. **39.♖g7+ ♔h6 40.♖ee7** 40...♖f8 41.♘f6!; 40...♘g6/e6 41.♖ef7; or 40...♖g6 41.♖h7+ ♔g5 42.♖e5+ ♔xg4 43.f3+ ♔xf3 44.♖f7. **40...♘xh5 41.g5** is a pretty mate!

9. Mamedyarov-Aronian
Paris 2018

Shakh could have saved himself by 31.♕xa6! ♖xa6 32.♖xe6!! (32.♖xa6? ♕xf3 33.♖xe6 ♕g4+) 32...♖xe6 33.♘g5+ ♔h6 34.♖c8! when Black has a choice between a drawn rook ending after 34...♕xg5+ and stalemate by 34...♖e8 35.♖xe8 ♕a1+ 36.♔g2 ♕h1+.

Hans Ree

Going digital

Recently, **HANS REE** was told that a sponsor of a small tournament in The Netherlands loved chess so much that he follows important games with 32 engines running to compare their evaluations. Though our columnist didn't really believe the story, it evoked memories of his own initiation into the digital age.

In June, during the blitz tournament in Leuven that was part of the Grand Chess Tour, I received an email from the Ukrainian grandmaster Mikhail Golubev, who wrote that in the game Aronian-Grischuk a move had been played that I had first played against David Levy in a tournament in Glasgow in 1973. It turned out to be 14...♖e8 in a line from the Velimirovic Attack. My move has scored badly in practice, and against Levy I had a narrow escape with a draw.

It would be flattering, but also rather unnerving, to presume that Golubev would know all my games by heart, even those that I had played when he was just three years old, but of course that was not the case. Last year, he had written a book about the Sicilian, mainly based on his own games, a big part of which was devoted to the Velimirovic Attack. He had just been checking for new developments in a line that interested him.

Nevertheless, I liked the fact that Golubev had come across my move. I told my wife about his email and she was mightily impressed. 'He mailed you about a move you played in 1973?

Really?' Nice people, these chess players, although a bit weird.

I tend to use my database as an old-fashioned photo album – to evoke memories. There are all these people I have crossed swords with. Quite a few have died. Many are just names for me now. Who were they and what did they look like? Sometimes there is a slight pang of regret, when I realize that in a distant past I have been insolent to innocent people, or, more banally, missed an easy win.

Sometimes I go to the database to ascertain the period when some important events in my private life happened. In what month did I finish my studies? It must have been just before the Olympiad in Siegen. The marriage of my best friend? A few months after the last Lone Pine tournament. Not all is lost to artificial memory. The date of my own marriage and everything that happened on that day I can remember without the crutches of the database. But if I ever forget, I can still have a look at the dates of the Olympiad in Lucerne.

Great times for reporters

The first time I used a computer was in 1986, when my newspaper lent me one

to take it to Dubai and report on the Olympiad, or rather on the election of a new FIDE president. The contenders were the sitting president Florencio Campomanes and the Brazilian Lincoln Lucena, who was a stooge of Raymond Keene and Garry Kasparov. I would have preferred to be there as a player, but the Dutch chess federation boycotted the event because Israel was not allowed to compete.

'I suppose you realize that we're not sending you to Dubai to report on the games', said the sports editor. I decided to smuggle in as much as possible about real chess, but there were stories to tell about the election, too. And in retrospect, these were golden days for our Dutch chess journalism, when I and my friend Gert Ligterink, who worked for a competing Dutch newspaper, were sent to Dubai, at considerable expense to our newspapers, to report on the election of a FIDE president. Chess was big then and newspapers had lots of money.

Gert had been an earlier adopter of the new technology, since he had brought a computer to previous assignments. We, his envious colleagues, called it the miracle machine.

In fact, in modern terms it could hardly be called a computer. It was a text processor with a communication program. The acoustic modem we used can hardly be described to youngsters, who may not even know what a traditional phone looked like. The modem was a big object with two rubber holes into which you had to shove the two ends of the handset of the telephone. Then you dialled the number of the computer at the other side, and if it worked, you heard the noises of data flow through the lines, a sound that is probably preserved in computer museums.

Trials and tribulations

It didn't always work smoothly, but in Dubai it did, as they had recently set up a modern communication infrastructure. Europe and, especially, the

me and these people of the hotel still working. It forged a bond.

I remember that during the match Kasparov-Timman in Prague in 1998, Gert Ligterink, who was staying in the same hotel as I, had to go to a public telephone booth every day to connect his computer and file his reports, but that was his own fault, because he should have changed the settings of his communication program.

Knight Gerald one to Ferdinand three

The pre-digital era had its problems, too. How to transmit a chess game over the phone? It went more or less like this: one knight Gerald one to Ferdinand three, Daniel seven to Daniel five, two Gerald two to Gerald three, etc. This was recorded on tape. The women (always women) who would type the

a palace revolt in the higher echelons of the company. The programmers left the good ship New In Chess to join the rebel prince of darkness to develop TascBase. New In Chess abandoned the field of databases to ChessBase.

Glued to the engines

I have worked with ChessBase 8 for the last 10 years, but over time my program was damaged and several functions stopped working. Recently, a good Samaritan gave me ChessBase 14, and everything works fine. But I must say I was rather discombobulated (see, Nigel, I can do this too). The new program can do everything I want, but also so much more that I do not want that I often still take refuge in good old version 8.

The German magazine *Schach* has a monthly interview in which one of the usual questions is: 'What do you think is the most harmful and what the best development in modern chess?' Often, the answer given to both questions is: the computer.

I must confess that I personally found the chess world before the advent of the engines more interesting. Call me a troglodyte if you will.

Recently, in the erstwhile Dutch fishermen's town of Spakenburg, I took part in a rapid tournament appropriately called the FishPartners Open. Among the participants were two computers, one of which was very strong. The strong computer won the tournament with 6½ out of 7. It did not compete for the money prizes, but it heavily influenced the distribution of prizes amongst the humans.

I was told that the main sponsor of that tournament is enamoured of chess engines, that he owned 32 different programs, and that this November, when the World Championship match will be on, he will follow the games and compare the evaluations of all of his 32 cyber-friends. I did not really believe this story, but if it is true, I take off my hat to such a splendidly mad obsession. ∎

'I tend to use my database as an old-fashioned photo album – to evoke memories.'

United States were hampered by the dialectics of progress, which says that when you think that you are comfortably ahead, you will be surpassed by newcomers who start out with the latest technology.

In these early years, my screen could handle 15 lines of text. It had no internal light, so we were dependent on a lamp in our hotel room. Sometimes you had to move to the bathroom.

Also, when you used the phone in your hotel room, there might be an automatic click that destroyed the connection with the computer back at the office.

I was working for a newspaper that appeared late in the afternoon, so I had all the time in the world, and in the early hours of the night I sometimes went to the communication headquarters of a hotel, from where they could send my article without a click. This was nice. Everybody asleep, just

game notation, were experienced chess handlers. If not, I would have had to indicate capitals, spaces, hyphens and dots at every move.

After going digital as a journalist it took a few years before I started using the computer as a player. First there was NICBase, which was developed around 1990. At first I hesitated. I found it complicated and with the slow computers of that time it took a while before you found the game you wanted to see.

'But think of all the time you save, the time you spend now browsing through magazines and books', said Wim Andriessen, the founding father of the New In Chess company. Of course he was right, even though browsing was more conducive to serendipity than clicking. While browsing, you will find things you had not been looking for.

Then, in 1993, NICBase folded as a commercial product. It had to do with

Jan Timman

Hammer blows in Helsingor

Jon-Ludvig Hammer was the deserved winner of the 2018 Xtracon Open. The Norwegian played a number of impressive games, including one that 'his friend Magnus Carlsen would have been proud of'. **JAN TIMMAN** reports from the summery get-together in Helsingor where GMs and amateurs from all corners of the world happily mix.

This summer, the Danish city of Helsingor once again held its gigantic open tournament, for the third time with Xtracon as the main sponsor. The event can count on continued sponsorship for the next three years. There have been editions with more than 400 players lining up, but this time there weren't quite that many. I myself played there for the seventh time, and I saw several familiar faces from the previous editions. Georgian grandmaster Baadur Jobava, last year's winner, was there again, as were Nikita Vitiugov (Russia) and Ivan Saric (Croatia). There was another possible winner: the 28-year-old Russian Dmitry Andreikin. Thirteen-year-old IM Vincent Keymer, Germany's big hope and the sensational winner of the Grenke Open earlier this year in Karlsruhe, also participated.

The tournament ran a curious course. The normal state of affairs is that halfway into the event, at most one player is leading with a perfect score. This time around, Norwegian GMs Simen Agdestein and Jon-Ludvig Hammer still had a perfect score after six rounds – a unique situation! Round 7 saw their inevitable personal clash. Hammer, as Black, came out of the

opening with all guns blazing, but then got himself into major trouble with an overly optimistic pawn sacrifice.

Simen Agdestein
Jon-Ludvig Hammer
Helsingor 2018 (7)

position after 46...♗b5

The time-trouble phase had ended a few moves earlier, but Agdestein still hadn't managed to find the winning continuation.

47.f4

Correct was 47.♖f7!, cutting off the black king. After 47...a4 48.d6 White will be there first.

47...a4 48.f5 a3 49.♖g6 ♗d3!

White must have missed this move. The f-pawn is pinned and will be lost.

50.♖g1 ♗xf5 51.♖a1 ♔b5 52.♖xa3 ♔c5 53.♖a6 ♗c8 54.d6 ♗d7 55.f3 b5 56.♖a8 ♔xd6 Draw.

Agdestein was clearly cut up by this missed opportunity, and in the next round he duly lost to young German GM Rasmus Svane, as good as scuppering his chances to fight for the highest honour. Hammer, on the other hand, took it easy, going for an early repetition in his Round 8 game as White against Vitiugov – a sound decision from a strategic point of view. There are no free days in Helsingor, so it doesn't hurt to create one yourself; and it also helped him to keep a dangerous rival at arm's length. In the final round, Hammer lashed out again, again as White.

Jon-Ludvig Hammer
Vincent Keymer
Helsingor 2018 (10)

Semi-Tarrasch

1.d4 ♘f6 2.c4 e6 3.♘f3 d5 4.♘c3 c5 5.cxd5 ♘xd5 6.g3
This fianchetto was introduced by Alekhine in the 24th game of his revenge match against Euwe in 1937.
6...cxd4 7.♘xd5 ♕xd5 8.♕xd4

Playing inspired chess and lashing out at the right moments, Norway's Jon-Ludvig Hammer won several key games to take first place in Helsingor.

8...♕b5
Tal's move. Euwe swapped on d4, but this failed to solve Black's opening problems. Better was 8...♘c6, as in Piket-Van Wely, Groningen 1997. After 9.♕xd5 exd5 10.♗g2 ♗f5 Black was pretty OK.
9.e4 ♕b4+ 10.♗d2 ♘c6 11.♕xb4 ♗xb4 12.♗b5 ♗d7 13.♖c1

'Norwegian GMs Agdestein and Hammer still had a perfect score after six rounds – a unique situation!'

13...f6 A safer option was 13...♗xd2+ 14.♔xd2 ♔e7, which, with a little transposition, would have led to Andersson-Portisch, Bazna 2008. After 15.♔e3 ♖ac8 16.♗xc6 ♗xc6 17.♖c3, Black should have gone 17...f6!, followed by advancing his e-pawn. Portisch, however, played 17...♗d7,

and after 18.♖hc1 ♖xc3+ 19.♖xc3 ♖c8 20.♖xc8 ♗xc8 21.e5 found himself in a difficult endgame, which Andersson went on to win in impressive fashion. Interestingly, Benko-Kortchnoi, Curaçao 1962, got to virtually the same endgame, which Kortchnoi also failed to hold.
14.♗xc6 ♗xd2+ 15.♔xd2 ♗xc6 16.♘d4 ♗xe4 17.♖he1 ♗d5 18.♘xe6 ♗xe6 19.♖xe6+

The double rook ending has arisen by force. Keymer sank into thought here.

19...♔f7!

The correct decision. The alternative 19...♔d7 would lead to a pawn ending almost by force after 20.♖e3! ♖ad8 21.♖d3+ ♔e6 22.♖c7 ♖xd3+ 23.♔xd3 ♖d8+ 24.♔c4 ♖d7 25.♖xd7 ♔xd7 26.♔d5. This position looks tenable because the white king will be unable to penetrate, but White can still make progress. Here are some lines to illustrate that White is winning.

ANALYSIS DIAGRAM

■ 26...h5 27.b4 g5 (27...a6 28.f4 g6 29.a4) 28.f4 gxf4 29.gxf4 ♔e7 30.b5 ♔d7 31.a4, and the a-pawn will run to a6, giving White two squares to penetrate from: c6 and e6. Black will find himself in zugzwang;
■ 26...♔e7 27.h4 ♔d7 28.h5 ♔e7 29.a4 ♔d7 30.b4 ♔e7 31.b5, and White will win in the same way.

20.♖d6 ♖hd8 21.♖c7+ ♔e8

This was the idea. Black is going for a favourable pawn ending.

22.♖d3

The best practical chance. After 22.♖xd8+ ♖xd8+ 23.♔e3 ♖d7 24.♖xd7 ♔xd7 25.♔d4 ♔d6 the pawn ending would be a lifeless affair.

22...♖xd3+ 23.♔xd3 ♖d8+ 24.♔c4 ♖d2 25.♖xb7 ♖xf2 26.a4 a5

27.b3 Cleverly played. Hammer is continuously setting his young opponent new tests.

27...♖xh2 28.♖xg7 ♖c2+ 29.♔b5 ♖b2 30.♔xa5 ♖xb3 31.g4 ♖e3

With 31...h6, Black could have aimed for a theoretically drawn endgame, but this was not easy to see. After 32.♔a6 ♖g3 33.a5 f5 34.♔b5 fxg4 35.a6 ♔f8 36.♖g6 ♔f7 37.a7 ♔xg6 38.a8♕ ♖f3 White will be unable to win. But the text is fine as well.

32.♖xh7

32...♖e5+?

But this loses a decisive tempo. Black should have brought his king closer to the white passed pawns. After 32...♔d8 33.♔b6 ♖e6+ 34.♔b7 ♖e5 35.♖h5 ♖e7+ 36.♔c6 ♖e6+ there is no win for White.

33.♔b6 ♖e6+ 34.♔b7 ♖e5 35.♖h5 ♖e7+ 36.♔c6 ♖e6+ 37.♔c7 Now

the white king has this extra square.
**37...♖e7+ 38.♔d6 ♖e4 39.a5
♖xg4 40.a6 ♖a4 41.♖h8+ ♔f7
42.a7** Black resigned.

Hammer played a few impressive
games in Helsingor. Against Saric
he consistently stuck to the theme of
domination.

**Jon-Ludvig Hammer
Ivan Saric**
Helsingor 2018 (6)
Sicilian Defence, Chameleon Variation

**1.e4 c5 2.♘c3 d6 3.♘ge2 ♘f6
4.h3 ♘c6 5.g4 d5 6.exd5 ♘xd5
7.♗g2 ♘xc3**

8.dxc3
In Naiditsch-Zhigalko, Minsk 2017,
White captured with the b-pawn, but
was worse in the middlegame. It is
better to go for an endgame here.
8...♕xd1+ 9.♔xd1 h5 10.gxh5

10...e5 A tad committal. 10...♖xh5
11.♘f4 ♖f5 looked better.
**11.♘g3 ♗e6 12.♔e2 0-0-0
13.♗e3 f5 14.♗g5 ♖e8**
And here, 14...♖d7 was correct. The
rook is too passive on e8.
15.h4 ♔c7

16.♗h3 Strong play. Black is forced to
concede square e4.
16...f4 After 16...♗c4+ 17.♔e1 ♗d5,
White would have made a strong
exchange sacrifice with 18.♗xf5!
♗xh1 19.♘xh1.
**17.♗xe6 ♖xe6 18.♘e4 ♖xh5
19.♖ad1 ♗e7 20.♔f3** It is time to
involve the king in the proceedings.
**20...b6 21.♔g4 g6 22.♖h3 c4
23.♖hh1 ♖h8**

24.h5 White could have postponed
the opening of the kingside by, for
example, advancing his b-pawn or
swapping on e7, but Hammer has correctly calculated that after the text
Black is still in trouble.
**24...♗xg5 25.♘xg5 gxh5+
26.♖xh5 ♖ee8 27.♘e6+ ♔c8
28.♖xh8 ♖xh8 29.♔f5 ♖h2 30.♖d2**

Test yourself

The following five exercises are based
on actual game positions from the
2018 Xtracon Open. The solutions
are given at the end of this article on
page 105.

Exercise 1

Hjartarson-Jobava (10)
position after 47.♖f4

Jobava was not in such blistering
form as last year, but he still managed
to clinch shared third place in the
final round.
Hjartarson has just played his rook
from b4 to f4. How did Black exploit
this?

Exercise 2

Andreikin-Tari (10)
position after 22...♘ab6

Also from the final round. And here,
too, it's about a combination based on
an undefended enemy piece.
How did Andreikin manage to catch
up in points with Hammer?

Exercise 3

Nakar-Berg (5)
position after 16...♖c8

Black has just put his rook on c8. Should White protect the c-pawn now?

Exercise 4

Foisor-Holm (9)
position after 19...♕b4

Black has just played his queen to b4. Should White go for the queen swap?

Exercise 5

Garberg-Timman (10)
position after 20...♖fe8

Where should White put his bishop?

Vincent Keymer scored his second GM norm. The 13-year-old German promise is developing into an interesting player with a keen sense for the initiative.

White has kept everything under control and can continue to reinforce his position.
30...b5 31.b4 a5 32.a3 axb4 33.axb4 ♖h3 34.♖d6 ♔b7 35.♘c5+ ♔c7 36.♘e4 ♖h4
A better defence was 36...♖h1.
37.♔e6 f3 38.♖d7+ ♔b8 39.♔d5
And White is still fully in control.
39...♘a7 40.♖f7 ♘c8

41.♖xf3 Harvest time. **41...♘e7+ 42.♔xe5 ♘g6+ 43.♔d4 ♘f4 44.♘d6 ♘d3+ 45.♔e3** Black resigned.

A game that Hammer's friend Magnus Carlsen would have been proud of.

Andreikin also won his last-round game, as I will show you below, but he had had clearly weaker opponents than Hammer, and was lagging considerably in Buchholz score, which meant that the Norwegian was declared the winner of the 2018 Xtracon Open.

For Keymer, the tournament ended very disappointingly, but it would have been hard to repeat his success in Karlsruhe, because he was Black in his last two games. That makes it virtually impossible to beat strong grandmasters. But he did score his second GM-result and will undoubtedly soon get the third one, as well as collecting the four rating points that separate him from the 2500 threshold.

Keymer is developing into an interesting player with a keen sense for the initiative. You can see this clearly in the following game.

Vincent Keymer
Allan Stig Rasmussen
Helsingor 2018 (8)
Benoni Defence

1.d4 ♞f6 2.c4 e6 3.♞f3 c5 4.d5
exd5 5.cxd5 d6 6.♞c3 g6 7.♝f4
♝g7 8.♛a4+ ♝d7 9.♛b3 ♛c7
10.e4 0-0 11.♞d2 ♞h5 12.♝e3 f5
13.exf5 ♝xf5

14.h3
The normal move here is the natural
developing move 14.♝e2. The text
was introduced by Riazantsev last
year. White wants to chase not only
the knight, but also the queen's bishop.
The drawback of this kingside expan-
sion is that Black will be able to play the
thematic advance ...b7-b5 unopposed.

14...♞f6
An interesting alternative was
14...♝xc3 15.♛xc3 ♞f6 16.♝c4 ♞bd7,
intending to guarantee active piece
play at the expense of the bishop pair.

15.g4 ♝d7 16.♝g2 ♞a6 17.0-0
♜ab8

18.♞de4
New. Riazantsev-Donchenko, Douglas
2017, saw 18.♜fe1 b5 19.♞ce4 here,
which boils down to virtually the same
thing.

18...♞xe4 19.♞xe4 b5 20.♜ac1
♛b6 It was not necessary to remove
the queen. Better was the immediate
20...♜be8.
21.a3 ♜be8 22.♜fe1 ♝e5 23.♔h1

The start of a sharp plan. White wants
to advance his f-pawn.

23...♛d8 24.♝g5 ♛b8 25.♝h6
♜f7 26.f4 c4

27.♛e3
Keymer plays it as sharply as possible,
sacrificing his b-pawn to get the
strongest initiative possible. With
27.♜xc4 bxc4 28.♛xb8 ♜xb8 29.fxe5
dxe5 30.♞d6, he could have gone for a
favourable endgame. But with 30...♞c5
Black can return the exchange, with
good chances of holding.

27...♝xb2 28.♜b1

Helsingor 2018

1	Jon-Ludvig Hammer	NOR 2631	8½
2	Dmitry Andreikin	RUS 2702	8½
3	Rasmus Svane	GER 2580	8
4	Nils Grandelius	SWE 2668	8
5	Marin Bosiocic	CRO 2589	8
6	Allan Stig Rasmussen	DEN 2536	8
7	Sune Berg Hansen	DEN 2584	8
8	Baadur Jobava	GEO 2644	8
9	Simen Agdestein	NOR 2581	7½
10	Vincent Keymer	GER 2466	7½
11	Ivan Saric	CRO 2689	7½
12	Nikita Vitiugov	RUS 2734	7½
13	Mads Andersen	DEN 2597	7½
14	Johan Salomon	NOR 2462	7½
15	Alexei Shirov	ESP 2637	7½
16	Benjamin Notkevich	NOR 2471	7½
17	Aryan Tari	NOR 2615	7½
18	Prantik Roy	IND 2347	7
19	Kassa Korley	DEN 2443	7
20	Sebastien Maze	FRA 2628	7
21	Axel Delorme	FRA 2515	7
22	Kristian Stuvik Holm	NOR 2453	7
23	Johann Hjartarson	ISL 2523	7
24	Chen Lin	CHN 2508	7
25	Boris Chatalbashev	DEN 2543	7
26	Elshan Moradiabadi	USA 2538	7
27	Karthik Venkataraman	IND 2514	7
28	Linus Johansson	SWE 2454	7
29	Jens Ingebretsen	NOR 2138	7
30	Jesper Sondergaard Thybo	DEN 2497	7
31	Grigor Grigorov	FID 2506	7
32	Christian Jepson	SWE 2410	7
33	Shiqun Ni	CHN 2435	7
34	Edward Song	USA 2275	7
35	Jonas Buhl Bjerre	DEN 2436	7
36	Ronan Le Goff	FRA 2295	7
37	Ralf Akesson	SWE 2397	7
38	Jonathan Carlstedt	GER 2425	7
39	Jan Timman	NED 2555	7
40	Milton Pantzar	SWE 2333	7
41	Olaf Berg	FAI 2226	7
42	Simon Bekker-Jensen	DEN 2483	6½
43	Ke Mu	CHN 2455	6½
44	Eylon Nakar	ISR 2462	6½
45	Jonny Hector	SWE 2499	6½
46	Frode Olav Olsen Urkedal	NOR 2552	6½
47	Sabina-Francesca Foisor	USA 2285	6½
48	Jakob Aabling-Thomsen	DEN 2379	6½
49	Craig Hilby	USA 2426	6½
50	Jacob Aagaard	SCO 2482	6½
	397 players, 10 rounds		

NEW!

The Full English Opening
Mastering the Fundamentals
Carsten Hansen   464 pages - €29.95

The first one-volume book on the popular English Opening that covers all variations.

"Currently the best guide in the market for this particular opening. Hansen has clearly put in an amazing amount of work into this book."
IM Kevin Goh Wein Ming

Bologan's Caro-Kann
A Modern Repertoire for Black
Victor Bologan   350 pages - €29.95

A complete repertoire that is much more than just a lucidly explained and highly playable set of responses. In many lines Bologan provides two options to handle the Black position. He presents lots of new ideas and resources. After reading and studying this book you are bound to win many exciting games with Bologan's Caro-Kann!

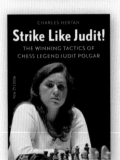

Strike like Judit!
The Winning Tactics of Chess Legend Judit Polgar
Charles Hertan   256 pages - €24.95

"Thanks to Hertan's well-written explanations, the reader too should be able to increase their own killer instinct."
CHESS Magazine (UK)

"Judit was a superb tactician, and the book collects her finest combinations."
GM Simen Agdestein, VG Daily Newspaper (Norway)

Winning in the Chess Opening
700 Ways to Ambush Your Opponent
Nikolay Kalinichenko   464 pages - €24.95

More than just a collection of traps and tricks. Kalinichenko always explains the ideas and plans behind the opening and how play could have been improved.

"Enjoyable, while also making the reader much more aware of where early pitfalls can suddenly spring from."
CHESS Magazine

Strategic Chess Exercises
Find the Right Way to Outplay Your Opponent
Emmanuel Bricard   224 pages - €24.95

"Bricard is clearly a very gifted trainer."
Grandmaster Daniel King

"For chess coaches this book is nothing short of phenomenal." – *Carsten Hansen, American Chess Magazine*

"A high-quality set of exercises that mimics quite well the decision-making process you go through in a game."
GM Matthew Sadler

Winning Chess Middlegames
An Essential Guide to Pawn Structures
Ivan Sokolov   288 pages - $29.95

A modern classic, finally back in print!

"Sokolov covers his material deeply, offering not glib generalities but very specific insights and explanations. Great Games, marvelous analysis."
Dennis Monokroussos, ChessToday

"Terrific instructional content and great games."
IM John Watson, The Week In Chess

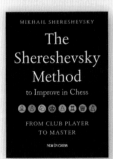

The Shereshevsky Method to Improve in Chess
From Club Player to Master
Mikhail Shereshevsky   352 pages - €27.95

"A must for all chess trainers and chess players who wish to improve their performance, because it covers all the skills a good chess player needs."
IM Dirk Schuh

"Well done, New In Chess! Now sign up the author for another book, as soon as possible."
Sean Marsh, CHESS Magazine

How Ulf Beats Black
Ulf Andersson's Bulletproof Strategic Repertoire for White
Cyrus Lakdawala   288 pages - €27.95

This repertoire will last a lifetime.

"There is a lot of good stuff to enjoy by exploring the ideas and openings of the Swedish legend."
IM Gary Lane, ECF Newsletter

"Lakdawala has come up with a 'not the usual fare, but definitely worth the detour' type of work. It's instructive, but not too heavy, so will suit all sorts."
GM Glenn Flear, Yearbook 127

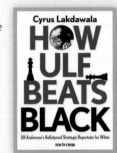

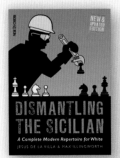

Dismantling the Sicilian – NEW EDITION
A Complete Modern Repertoire for White
Jesus de la Villa & Max Illingworth 368 pages - €27.95

"Many novelties and improvements on existing theory have been added."
Carsten Hansen, author of 'The Chameleon Sicilian'

"Novelties abound. A high-quality and durable repertoire that has the potential to cause significant theoretical and practical problems."
Paul Hopwood, CHESS Magazine

My System & Chess Praxis
His Landmark Classics in One Edition
Aron Nimzowitsch   576 pages – €26.95

Includes 'The Blockade' and 'On the History of the Chess Revolution'.

"This translation finally allows English-speaking audiences to acquaint themselves with the real Nimzowitsch."
Jeremy Silman, author of 'How to Reassess Your Chess'

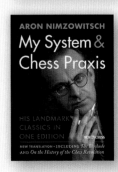

28...♗h8

Most players would have gone for this, but 28...♗f6!, trying to hinder the white initiative on the kingside as best as possible, would have been stronger. After 29.f5 gxf5 30.gxf5 ♔h8 31.♗f4 ♗e5, Black will be able to hold.

29.f5 ♕d8 30.♕f2

Simpler was 30.fxg6 hxg6 31.♖f1, with advantage, but White has a more complicated plan.

30...♖xe4

An understandable exchange sacrifice. Black wants to relieve the pressure on his position. The alternative was 30...♗e5. After 31.♘g5 gxf5 32.♘xf7 ♔xf7 33.♖xe5 ♖xe5 34.♗f4 White maintains his pressure on the enemy position, but with nothing decided yet.

31.♖xe4 ♘c5 32.♖e6!

The point of the white play.

32...♘d3

Now Black will meet an inglorious end. It was absolutely necessary to take the rook. After 32...♘xe6 33.dxe6 ♗xe6 34.♕e2 ♗d7 35.♗d5

ANALYSIS DIAGRAM

Black has the following options:
■ 35...♕h4 36.♕e3 ♗e5 37.♔g2 gxf5 38.♖f1 (38.♗g5 can be met by 38...f4) 38...♗d4!, and Black will probably just scrape home. A difficult variation to find;
■ 35...♕e8 36.♕g2 (the queen swap won't yield much: 36.♕xe8+ ♗xe8 37.♗f4 ♗c3, and Black holds) 36...♗f6 37.♖f1 g5 38.h4, and the white initiative continues unabated.

33.♕e3 gxf5 34.gxf5 ♗e5 35.♗e4

Freeing the way for the rook.

35...♗xe6 36.dxe6 ♖c7 37.♗d5 ♔h8 38.♖g1 ♕h4 39.♖g8+

Black resigned.

My own tournament never took off after I blundered a piece in Round 2 (a morning round). This left me in the upper regions of the Konventum conference centre, where the lesser gods usually battle it out. The atmosphere there was clearly more relaxed. This reminded me of the fact that the Xtracon Open is not only a grandmasterly fight for the highest honour, but also a summery get-together of amateurs from all corners of the world.

Solution 1

Black won with **47...♖h2+!** The rook sac is based on the white queen being unprotected. **48.♔f1 ♖f2+! 49.♔xf2 ♘g4+** And White resigned. He will lose his queen.

Solution 2

White won with **23.♘3d4** He could also have captured on f7 first. **23...exd4 24.♗xf7+!** The point of the previous move. The black rook is unprotected. **24...♔xf7 25.♕h5+ ♔g8 26.♕xe8** And Black resigned. He cannot prevent the fatal check on e7.

Solution 3

White left the pawn hanging and continued: **17.f6!** Aiming for d7. **17...♕xc2+ 18.♔a1 ♕xe4 19.fxg7 ♗xg7** And now **20.♘c3!** would have been the decisive blow, with the point **20...♕c6 21.♘e4 d5 22.♘a5** and wins.
The game went 20.♘b6 ♖c7 21.♖xd7, after which Black could have saved his skin with 21...♗c8!.

Solution 4

Yes. With **20.♕xb4 ♗xb4 21.♗xa6!** White could have grabbed the advantage. Black must go all out not to lose a pawn. After **21...bxa6 22.♘a2, 22...♗d2!** is the only move, but White retains his positional plus after **23.♖xd2 ♗xa4 24.♘b4**
In the game, White avoided the swap, after which Black was OK.

Solution 5

He should have returned his bishop to d2 in order to protect the queen's knight. But there followed **21.♗f2? ♘g4! 22.0-0 ♘xf2 23.♖xf2 ♖ab8 24.♖c1 ♘b3 25.♖b1 ♘d4 26.♖ff1 ♖b4** And Black was winning. ■

Cristian Chirila

AUSTIN FUELLER

CURRENT ELO: 2576

DATE OF BIRTH: January 6, 1991

PLACE OF BIRTH: Bucharest, Romania

PLACE OF RESIDENCE: Columbia MO, United States

What is your favourite city?
I was thoroughly impressed by Positano on Italy's Amalfi Coast.

What was the last great meal you had?
In the heart of Rome, with my girlfriend, a bottle (or more) of Malbec, Penne all'Arrabbiata, and live music.

What drink brings a smile to your face?
A freshly brewed cup of coffee in the morning.

Which book would you give to a dear friend?
Sapiens by Yuval Harari.

Which book are you currently reading?
Skin in the Game by Nicholas Taleb, *Guns, Germs, and Steel* by Fred Diamond, *Ali: A Life* by Jonathan Eig.

What is your all-time favourite movie?
Pulp Fiction.

And your favourite TV series?
True Detective is on the top of my list.

What music do you listen to?
I'm a big fan of Techno and Rap, generally switching between these depending on the 'zone' I'm in.

Who is your favourite chess player of all time?
I did not study the classics enough to have a pertinent opinion.

Is there a chess book that had a profound influence on you?
I grew up as a computer kid, but since I became a coach, I have found Dvoretsky's books incredibly insightful. The mix between psychology, personal stories, and amazing examples make any of his books a classic.

What was your best result ever?
Becoming U-16 World Youth Champion. But winning the U-2550 section of Millionaire Chess gave me a lot of confidence, that helped me improve many facets of my life.

And the best game you played?
My victory against Alex Shimanov (U-16 Team Olympiad) I'll always remember.

Do chess players have typical shortcomings?
A lot of chess players have a difficult time adjusting to life outside of the chess bubble, myself included.

Do you have any superstitions concerning chess?
I find new superstitions every tournament. A favourite pen, a favourite time to work out, the list could go on forever...

Facebook, Instagram, Snapchat, or?
Twitter is the one I'm most addicted to.

How many friends do you have on Facebook?
1600.

Who do you follow on Twitter?
Chess professionals and cryptocurrency degenerates.

What is your life motto?
Right now I'm in the 'The world doesn't owe you anything' phase.

When were you happiest?
I don't do well dwelling on the past. Right now I'm happiest.

When was the last time you cried?
I always have a weak moment a few days before I travel back to Romania to see my family, usually when driving and that one song comes on.

Which three people would you like to invite for dinner?
Marcus Aurelius, Bruce Lee, Jordan Peterson.

What is the best piece of advice you were ever given?
I don't do well with advice coming from other people; I try to understand things through experience.

Is there something you'd love to learn?
I'm addicted to martial arts, and would love to master Jiu Jitsu.

What is your greatest fear?
Growing old is always a difficult reality to face. Right now my biggest fear is allowing myself to become complacent.

And your greatest regret?
Starting smoking at a young age (constantly flirting with the idea of quitting). There has been no upside to that habit.

What does it mean to be a chess player?
I view chess as an incredible world of opportunity. I am not only a player. I am a coach, commentator and much more.

Is a knowledge of chess useful in everyday life?
100%.

What is the best thing that was ever said about chess?
Can't think of anything as flattering as to be worth mentioning.